BUSINESS ISSUES, COMPETITION AND ENTREPRENEURSHIP

FEDERAL EMPLOYEES AND SEXUAL ORIENTATION IN THE WORKPLACE

POLICY, PERCEPTION, AND PROTECTIONS

BUSINESS ISSUES, COMPETITION AND ENTREPRENEURSHIP

Additional books in this series can be found on Nova's website under the Series tab.

Additional e-books in this series can be found on Nova's website under the e-book tab.

BUSINESS ISSUES, COMPETITION AND ENTREPRENEURSHIP

FEDERAL EMPLOYEES AND SEXUAL ORIENTATION IN THE WORKPLACE

POLICY, PERCEPTION, AND PROTECTIONS

ROSS HENDERSON
EDITOR

nova publishers
New York

Library of Congress Cataloging-in-Publication Data

ISBN: 978-1-63484-376-8

Published by Nova Science Publishers, Inc. † New York

CONTENTS

Preface		**vii**
Chapter 1	Sexual Orientation and the Federal Workplace *U.S. Merit Systems Protection Board*	**1**
Chapter 2	Update on State Statutes and Administrative Complaint Data on Employment Discrimination Based on Sexual Orientation and Gender Identity *U.S. Government Accountability Office*	**63**
Chapter 3	Sexual Orientation and Gender Identity Discrimination in Employment: A Legal Analysis of the Employment Non-Discrimination Act (ENDA) *Jody Feder and Cynthia Brougher*	**91**
Index		**107**

PREFACE

Prior to 1975, Federal Government policy considered an individual's sexual orientation when determining suitability for Federal employment. Although we will never know the exact number of individuals who were denied employment or who had their employment terminated based on their actual or assumed sexual orientation, one estimate places this number between 7,000 and 10,000 in the 1950's alone. Federal law now prohibits discrimination in employment based on a number of factors, including race, color, religion, sex, national origin, disability, and age. This book examines sexual orientation and gender identity discrimination in employment, and provides policies, perception, and protections against discrimination in the workplace.

In: Federal Employees and Sexual Orientation ISBN: 978-1-63484-376-8
Editor: Ross Henderson

Chapter 1

SEXUAL ORIENTATION AND THE FEDERAL WORKPLACE*

U.S. Merit Systems Protection Board

THE CHAIRMAN

U.S. MERIT SYSTEMS PROTECTION BOARD
1615 M Street, NW
Washington, DC 20419-0001

The President
President of the Senate
Speaker of the House of Representatives

Dear Sirs:

In accordance with the requirements of 5 U.S.C. § 1204(a)(3), it is my honor to submit this U.S. Merit Systems Protection Board (MSPB) report, *Sexual Orientation and the Federal Workplace: Policy and Perception*. The purpose of our study was to examine Federal employee perceptions of workplace treatment based on sexual orientation, review how Federal

* This is an edited, reformatted and augmented version of a report to the President and Congress, issued May 2014.

workplace protections from sexual orientation discrimination evolved, and determine if further action is warranted to communicate or clarify those protections.

Since 1980, the U.S. Office of Personnel Management has interpreted the tenth Prohibited Personnel Practice (5 U.S.C. § 2302(b)(10)), which bars discrimination in Federal personnel actions based on conduct that does not adversely affect job performance, to prohibit sexual orientation discrimination. As this prohibition has neither been specifically expressed in statute nor affirmed in judicial decision, it has been subject to alternate interpretations. Executive Order 13087 prohibited sexual orientation discrimination in Federal employment but provided no enforceable rights or remedies for Federal employees who allege they are the victims of sexual orientation discrimination.

Any ambiguity in the longstanding policy prohibiting sexual orientation discrimination in the Federal workplace would be resolved by legislation making that prohibition explicit. Such legislation could grant Federal employees who allege they are victims of sexual orientation discrimination access to the same remedies as those who allege discrimination on other bases.

Federal employee respondents to MSPB surveys perceived that sexual orientation discrimination occurred about as often as discrimination based on national origin and marital status or violations of veteran's preference. Lesbian, gay, bisexual, and transgender (LGBT) Federal employee perceptions of the workplace are generally less positive than their colleagues. We found, however, that in some agencies for at least some issues, LGBT employee perceptions were as positive as those of other employees. We recommend that Federal agencies review their management policies to ensure they are inclusive and fair to all employees and that agencies better communicate the prohibitions against sexual orientation discrimination in the Federal workplace.

Respectfully,
Susan Tsui Grundmann

Enclosure

EXECUTIVE SUMMARY

Background

Prior to 1975, Federal Government policy considered an individual's sexual orientation when determining suitability for Federal employment. Although we will never know the exact number of individuals who were denied employment or who had their employment terminated based on their actual or assumed sexual orientation, one estimate places this number between 7,000 and 10,000 in the 1950's alone. It is impossible to determine the number of individuals who may not have sought Federal employment due to the knowledge that their sexual orientation made them ineligible for selection.

The tenth Prohibited Personnel Practice (PPP) (5 U.S.C. § 2302(b)(10)) codified in 1978 bars discrimination in Federal personnel actions based on conduct that does not adversely affect job performance. This prohibition was first interpreted to bar sexual orientation discrimination in 1980 by the U.S. Office of Personnel Management (OPM). As this prohibition has been neither specifically expressed in statute nor affirmed in judicial decision, it has been subject to alternate interpretations.

An executive order signed in 1998 affirmed the policy of non-discrimination based on sexual orientation in Federal employment. As this executive order was only a statement of policy, it provided no enforceable rights for employees who believed they had been discriminated against due to their sexual orientation.

In 2012, OPM's annual Federal Employee Viewpoint Survey (FEVS) for the first time asked Federal employees to self-identify their sexual orientation. The resulting large-scale data set presents an opportunity to examine lesbian, gay, bisexual, and transgender[1] (LGBT) employee perceptions of the Federal workplace for the first time.

Study Purpose

The purpose of MSPB's inquiry was to:

- Review the evolution of Federal employment policy based on sexual orientation;
- Examine the perceptions of Federal employees of workplace treatment based on sexual orientation;

- Examine the perceptions of LGBT Federal employees of their workplace and how these perceptions differ, if at all, from perceptions of other employees; and
- Determine if further action is warranted to communicate or clarify Federal workplace protections from sexual orientation discrimination.

Findings

There are encouraging signs that the history of sexual orientation discrimination discussed in this report is being overcome. For example, LGBT employees appear to be represented in the supervisory, managerial, and executive ranks in the same proportion as they are in the overall Federal workforce. In addition, similar percentages of heterosexual and LGBT Federal employees agree that PPPs are not tolerated in the workplace.

Federal Employee Perceptions of Sexual Orientation Discrimination

In a 2010 MSPB survey of Federal employees, three percent of respondents reported that sexual orientation discrimination had occurred in their workplace. This was a similar percentage of employees who perceived other PPP's had occurred including discrimination based on national origin or marital status and violations of veteran's preference laws. An additional one percent of respondents to the survey reported being the direct target of sexual orientation discrimination.

As we would expect, employees who perceived themselves to be the target of such discrimination were far less engaged in their work than other employees. Employees who perceived such discrimination had occurred but were not personally affected by the discrimination were also less engaged in their work than employees who did not believe such discrimination had occurred. That sexual orientation discrimination may affect individuals beyond the direct targets of such discrimination reinforces the importance of keeping the workplace free from this practice.

In response to the 2010 MSPB survey, 81 percent of supervisory respondents and 68 percent of non-supervisory respondents agreed that their organizations have made it clear that they prohibit sexual orientation discrimination. This means that almost one-fifth of supervisors and almost one-third of non-supervisors did not agree that their agencies have made it clear that they prohibit discrimination based on sexual orientation.

LGBT Federal Employee Perceptions of the Workplace

OPM has previously reported that, according to 2012 FEVS results, LGBT Federal employee perceptions of the workplace are generally less positive than those of other employees. Our further analysis of 2012 FEVS data revealed that, in some agencies for at least some workplace issues LGBT employee perceptions were as positive about the workplace as those of their heterosexual colleagues. This suggests that agencies may be able to create more inclusive cultures, resulting in a more positive atmosphere in the workplace.

Recommendations

Although the interpretation that the tenth PPP prohibits sexual orientation discrimination in the Federal workplace has been generally accepted, it remains an interpretation. Any ambiguity in the longstanding policy prohibiting sexual orientation discrimination would be resolved by legislation making that prohibition explicit. Such legislation could grant Federal employees who allege they are victims of sexual orientation discrimination access to the same remedies as those who allege discrimination on other bases.

Given the differences we found in workplace perceptions between LGBT and heterosexual employees within different agencies, agencies should review their management programs, policies, and procedures to ensure that they are inclusive and fair to all employees. The disparity we found among different groups of employees regarding the extent to which they believe their organization has made it clear that it prohibits sexual orientation discrimination suggests that agencies can improve their communication of that prohibition to employees.

HISTORICAL FOUNDATIONS: DISCRIMINATION TO ACCOMMODATION

This Section summarizes the institutionalized sexual orientation discrimination that Federal employees experienced in the past. We begin with this historical view to educate the Federal employees who may be unaware of this history. The following Section outlines the steps that have been taken to correct these discriminatory employment policies.

Background

Although the public campaign against employing gays and lesbians in the Federal civil service during the 1950's and 1960's may be the best known example of sexual orientation discrimination in Federal employment, that era certainly was not the beginning of such discrimination. For instance, the founder of the earliest documented homosexual[2] rights organization in America was dismissed from the Post Office Department in 1925 for being homosexual.[3]

By the middle of the twentieth century, the Federal Government had long required its employees to be of good moral character—a standard that excluded known homosexuals,[4] who were commonly referred to during this period as "sexual perverts" or "moral perverts."[5] Homosexuality was classified as a mental disorder by the American Psychiatric Association until it was removed from its Diagnostic and Statistical Manual of Mental Disorders in 1973.[6]

In the 1950's, many highly-placed Government and political leaders of both major parties believed that sexual subversion paralleled political subversion. For example, in a 1950 newsletter, the Republican National Chairman asserted that "sexual perverts" who had infiltrated the Government were "perhaps as dangerous as the actual Communists." The Chairman said he was elevating the "homosexual angle" to the national political level partially due to the difficulties encountered by newspapers and other commentators "in adequately presenting the facts while respecting the decency of their American audience." If not for these difficulties, "the country would be more aroused over this tragic angle."[7]

Some officials believed the country was already very concerned. In July 1950, three of President Truman's top advisors warned him that the country was more concerned about homosexuals in the Federal civil service than about Communists.[8] Perhaps the country had been paying attention to the debates in Congress, where the issue was frequently discussed on both the House and Senate floors. The issue received so much Congressional attention that one Congressman commented, "I do not know what homosexuals are, but I never saw anybody get as much free advertising in the Congress of the United States in all of my life."[9]

Federal Bureau of Investigation (FBI) Director J. Edgar Hoover also associated communism with homosexuality. According to one historian, the connection seemed self-evident to Director Hoover—both Communists and homosexuals "had clandestine and compartmented lives. They inhabited secret underground communities. They used coded language. Hoover believed, as did his peers, that both were uniquely susceptible to sexual entrapment and blackmail by foreign intelligence services."[10]

These beliefs were undoubtedly fueled by the exposure of a Soviet spy ring within the British intelligence and diplomatic services in 1951. The five members of the ring had been recruited by the Soviet Union while they were either teachers or students at Cambridge University in the 1930's and had risen to important posts in the British Government during World War II. Some of the group were stationed in America with access to the Central Intelligence Agency (CIA) and the Pentagon. When the first two members of the ring were exposed, they were able to disappear behind the Iron Curtain. Two of the group were homosexual and one was bisexual.[11]

Consequently, anti-homosexual fervor was fed by the fear of Communism which laid the groundwork for the purges of homosexual employees within the Federal civilian service, beginning in earnest in 1950 and continuing throughout the Cold War.[12] Examples of the efforts of both the legislative and executive branches to rid the civil service of homosexuals are discussed below, as is the judicial response to those efforts. (See **Figure 1** for a timeline of the events that are discussed in this report.)

Legislative Investigation

The Subcommittee on Investigations, Senate Committee on Expenditures in the Executive Departments, released a report entitled *Employment of Homosexuals and Other Sex Perverts in Government*[13] in December 1950. That inquiry was spurred in part by the testimony of a State Department official earlier that year before a Senate appropriations subcommittee that 91 "sex perverts" had been allowed to resign from that Department in the previous 3 years.[14] The Subcommittee on Investigations was alarmed to discover that some of these employees had actually found employment with other Federal agencies.

The Subcommittee on Investigations had three objectives in launching their inquiry: (1) to determine the number of homosexuals and other "sex perverts" employed by the Government; (2) to consider reasons why homosexuals were unsuitable for employment; and (3) to examine whether the methods used to keep homosexuals out of Government jobs were effective.[15] The subcommittee findings in these three areas are summarized below.

Number of Homosexuals Employed

At the time of the Subcommittee on Investigations' report, the U.S. Civil Service Commission (CSC) functioned as the centralized personnel management instrument of the Federal civilian service. CSC regulations had been in effect for many years providing that "criminal, infamous, dishonest, immoral or notoriously disgraceful conduct, which include[d] homosexuality, or other types of sex perversion," were sufficient grounds for denying appointment to, or removing individuals from, the Federal service.[16]

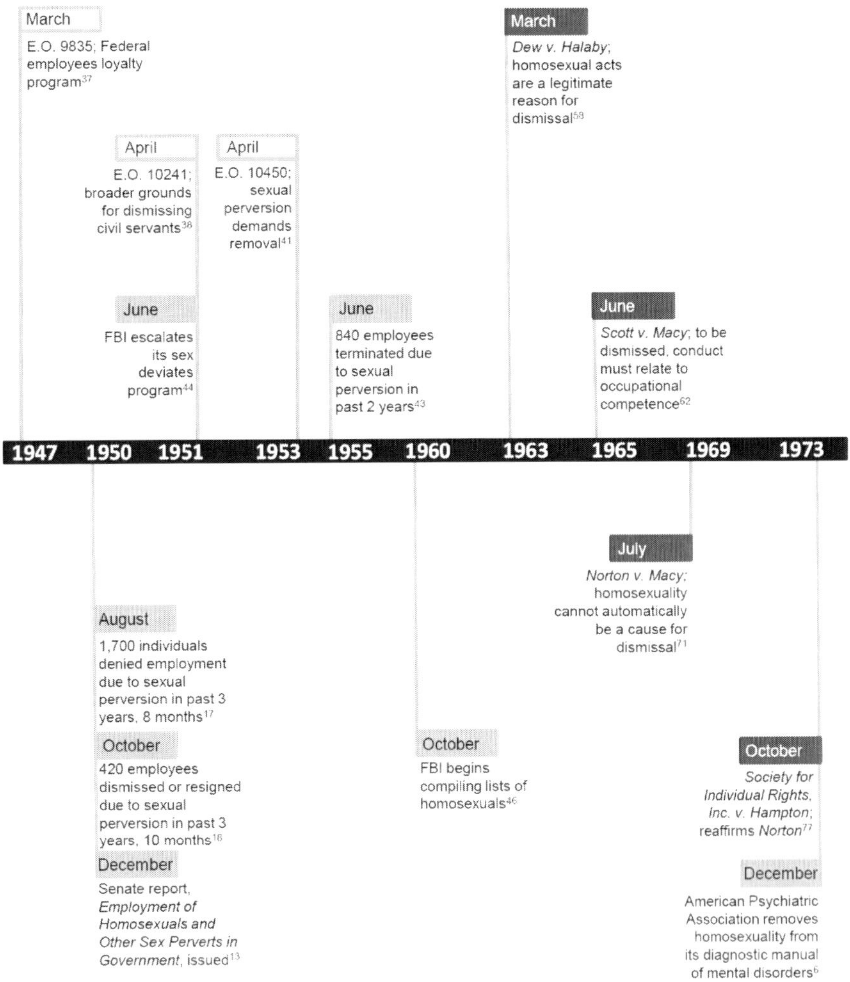

Figure 1. (Continued)

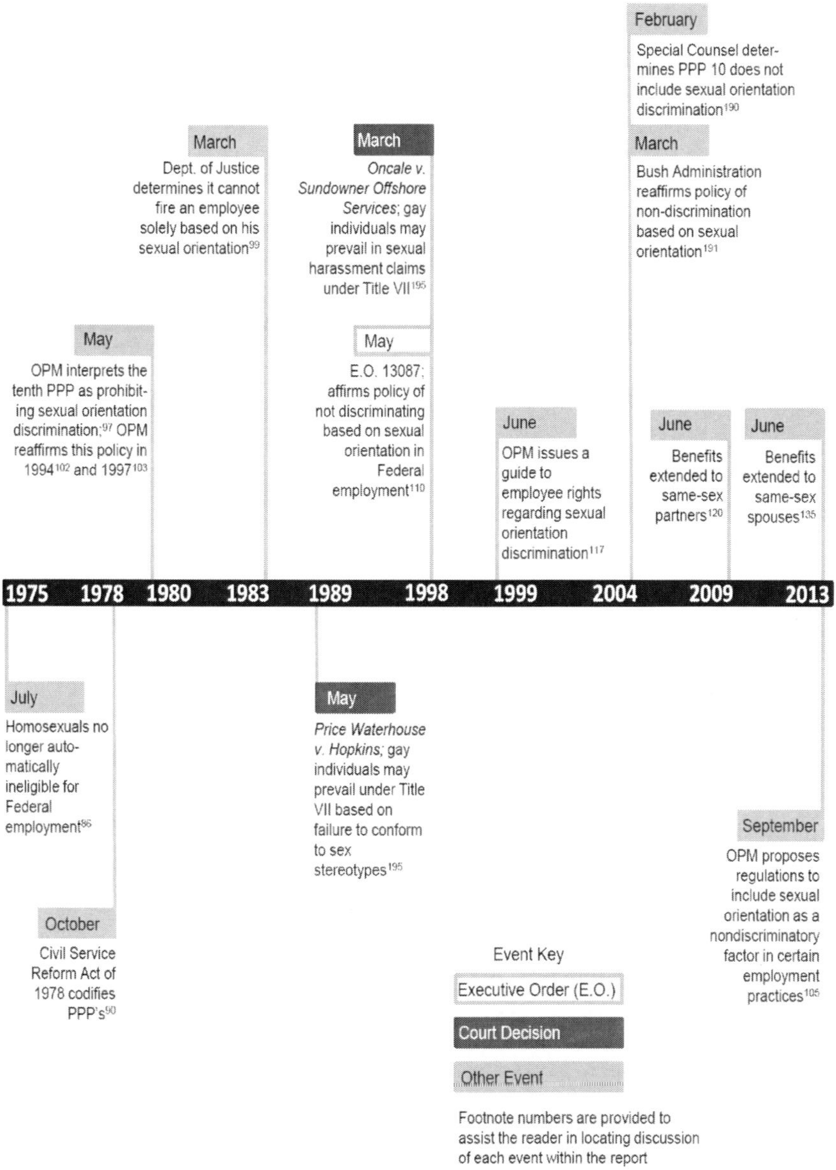

Figure 1. Timeline of major events discussed in this report.

Based on these regulations, according to CSC records, the Subcommittee on Investigations inquiry revealed that between January 1947 and August 1950 approximately 1,700 applicants were denied Federal employment because they had a record of homosexuality or other "sex perversion."[17] In addition, from January 1947 through October 1950 civilian agencies handled 574 cases involving charges of homosexuality or other types of "sex perversion" among Federal employees. Of these 574 employees, 207 had been dismissed and 213 had resigned from Federal employment. The remainder of the cases were either pending or the charges were not substantiated.[18]

The subcommittee report took Federal agencies to task for not addressing the issue of homosexuals in the Federal service more proactively. Of the 574 cases mentioned above, only 192 arose in the 3 years prior to the widespread publicity given to the issue by the appropriations subcommittee in April 1950. In the 7 months after those hearings, 382 cases were handled. According to the subcommittee, "These figures clearly indicate[d] that many of the civilian agencies of the Government were either negligent or otherwise failed to discover many of the homosexuals in their employ until after this situation was brought to light as the result of Congressional action."[19]

Suitability of Homosexuals

The Subcommittee on Investigations determined that "homosexuals and other sex perverts were not proper persons to be employed in Government for two reasons—first, they [were] generally unsuitable, and second, they constitute[d] security risks."[20] Much rhetoric revolved around the security risk it was believed that homosexuals posed to the Government. Experts testified before Congress that "moral perverts" were bad security risks because they were susceptible to blackmail due to the threat of exposure of their moral weakness.[21] Even absent security issues, the subcommittee report indicated it believed that homosexuals were inherently unsuitable for Federal employment.

In describing the unsuitability of homosexuals for Government employment, the Subcommittee on Investigations asserted that it was generally believed that those who engaged in acts of perversion lacked the emotional stability of other persons and those perversions weakened the moral fiber to such an extent that they were not suitable for positions of responsibility.[22] In addition, the subcommittee believed homosexuals tended to surround themselves with other homosexuals, and if such a person were to attain a position where he could influence hiring in the Federal service, "it is almost inevitable that he will attempt to place other homosexuals in Government jobs."[23] Finally, the subcommittee's investigation concluded that "perverts will frequently attempt to entice normal individuals to engage in perverted practices," and other employees should not be subjected to such influences while in Government service.[24] In short, "One homosexual can pollute a Government office."[25]

Some questioned whether homosexuals alone deserved this intense focus, given that many people could be deemed unsuitable for Federal service based either on security or general concerns. In a series of *New York Post* articles in July 1950, the Senate Minority Leader examined this topic. When told that some observers would consider promiscuous heterosexuals security risks, or that reckless gamblers or alcoholics might be entangled by blackmail, the Senator responded, "You can stretch the security risk further if you want to, but right now I want to start with the homosexuals. When we get through with them, then we'll see what comes next."[26]

Methods to Keep Homosexuals Out of the Civil Service

According to the Subcommittee on Investigations, Federal agencies were not doing enough to remove "sex perverts" from the civil service for a variety of reasons. The subcommittee contended that agencies and personnel officers were acting without regard to the CSC rules, there was confusion about how such cases should be handled, and some officials actually condoned employing homosexuals, especially in cases where their activities were carried out in ways that did not result in public scandal or notoriety. It was the subcommittee's determination that officials who adopted this last viewpoint "based their conclusions on the false premise that what a Government employee did outside of the office on his own time, particularly if his actions did not involve his fellow employees or his work, was his own business."[27]

One of the CSC rules that agencies were apparently disregarding was the requirement that the real reason that an employee resigned or was dismissed be recorded in the employee's personnel file. Some agencies that fired or removed homosexuals concealed the fact that such persons were hired in the first place by not noting the real reason for their dismissal in the personnel file—nor did the agencies notify the CSC (as required) of the real reason for the dismissal. Thus, a homosexual might be forced out of one department but remain able to obtain employment in another. The subcommittee noted that the CSC had recently expanded its program of inspecting agency personnel files to prevent this type of violation.[28]

A method that the Subcommittee on Investigations identified as being underused in the effort to prevent the employment of homosexuals in the Federal Government was the use of police records to identify such persons. During the 1960's, 49 of the 50 States prohibited private, consensual homosexual activity—only Illinois allowed such conduct between adults.[29]

The subcommittee noted that the FBI had recently obtained all available police records of persons charged with perverted sex offenses within the District of Columbia and furnished that information to the CSC. In addition, the FBI had begun furnishing to the CSC the criminal records of all persons arrested throughout the country on charges of sex perversion who were known to be Federal civil servants. The CSC then forwarded the information to the employing agencies and followed up with the agencies to determine what action had been taken in each case.[30]

The question of whether homosexual Federal employees were being dismissed solely for breaking laws is a difficult one. As we have seen, the major issues the subcommittee seemed to have with homosexual employees centered on security risk and general unsuitability—not law breaking. Criminal conduct was certainly a basis for disqualification from Federal employment, but the CSC applied this standard based on public mores. For example, as recently as 1969, the CSC declined to apply the standard to fornication and adultery because it believed a large portion of society did not regard these offenses as morally repugnant.[31] Likewise, the CSC investigated lesbianism less vigorously than male homosexuality because, in the CSC's opinion, the public found lesbianism considerably less repugnant.[32] In any event, Federal employees in Illinois (where homosexual acts between consenting adults had been decriminalized) were also disqualified from the civil service. Therefore, the fact that homosexual acts were criminalized does not seem to be the controlling factor that barred participants in such acts from Federal employment.[33]

Although the subcommittee report pointed out that the CSC and other Federal agencies were to follow certain procedures in removing "sex perverts" or other undesirable employees from the Federal service, the hysteria of the era is evident in one of its conclusions:

> There is no place in the United States Government for persons who violate the laws or the accepted standards of morality, or who otherwise bring disrepute to the Federal service by infamous or scandalous personal conduct. Such persons are not suitable for Government positions and in the case of doubt the American people are entitled to have errors of judgment on the part of their officials, if there must be errors, resolved on the side of caution.[34]

Even though this particular investigation resulted only in a more efficient bureaucratic response and not additional legislation barring homosexuals from Federal employment does not mean that Congress never used the power of legislation to prod the bureaucratic efforts along. As early as 1946, Congress had attached what came to be known as "McCarran riders" to agency appropriations bills. This gave the heads of those agencies absolute discretion to dismiss any Federal employee if it was "deemed necessary in the interest of national security." Adding McCarran riders to some agency appropriations was specifically designed to help those agencies remove homosexuals.[35] In 1950 Congress extended this summary dismissal power to 11 Federal agencies and authorized the President to extend it further if he deemed necessary.[36]

Civil Service Policy

Pressure to rid the civil service of homosexuals also emanated from within the executive branch. In response to this pressure, efforts to purge homosexual employees increased with prominent roles played by the CSC and the FBI. A brief overview of these CSC and FBI efforts will be examined below, after a discussion of the executive orders that came to require those efforts.

Executive Orders

The effort to weed disloyal or subversive persons out of the civil service began on March 21, 1947, when President Truman signed Executive Order 9835, *Prescribing Procedures for the Administration of an Employees Loyalty Program in the Executive Branch of the Government*. This executive order prompted the largest Government investigation up to that point in American history. In implementing Executive Order 9835, the FBI ran background checks on more than two million Government employees. It launched deep investigations into the personal lives and political beliefs of more than 14,000 of those employees. The program would unearth no Soviet spies in the Government, but the hunt for the disloyal and subversive spread throughout the American political system.[37]

Under pressure from those in Congress who believed he was soft on Communists in the Government, President Truman issued Executive Order 10241 in April 1951, which made it easier to question a civil servant's loyalty, and thus easier to remove them.[38] Previously, under Executive Order 9835, to dismiss an individual, there had to be "reasonable grounds for belief that the person [was] disloyal." Under Executive Order 10241, there only had to be a "reasonable doubt" of loyalty. The earlier order implied the need for an official to have an actual belief of disloyalty, while the latter order only required some doubt, without that doubt rising to the level of belief.[39] Nearly

3,000 Federal employees who had been cleared under the old standard had their cases reopened as a result of this new standard.[40]

Two years later, President Eisenhower instituted a stringent standard for retention in Executive Order 10450, *Security Requirements for Government Employees*, which he signed on April 27, 1953. He ordered that the Federal Government could only employ and retain employees when it was "clearly consistent with the interests of national security." Executive Order 10450 also, for the first time, listed sexual perversion as a condition that demanded removal from the Federal service.[41] During the first year that Executive Order 10450 was in effect, 618 civil servants were terminated or resigned in accordance with its requirements due to sex perversion.[42] An additional 222 Federal employees were terminated or resigned due to sex perversion during the second year that the executive order was in effect.[43]

Federal Bureau of Investigation Activities

To deal with the perceived threat that homosexuals posed to the Government, the FBI escalated its Sex Deviates Program in mid-1951. As part of this program, the FBI contacted universities and police departments across the country to alert them to the subversive homosexual threat. They sought to drive "homosexuals from every institution of government, higher learning, and law enforcement in the nation. The FBI's files on American homosexuals grew to 300,000 pages over the next 25 years before they were destroyed."[44]

At an October 1960 National Security Council meeting, President Eisenhower spent almost an hour discussing with Director Hoover how the Government could be cleansed of the homosexual threat once and for all. The meeting followed closely on the heels of the defection of two National Security Agency (NSA) code breakers to the Soviet Union. The code breakers were rumored to be homosexuals—an assumption that was unsupported by NSA records declassified 50 years later. At the meeting, it was agreed that the FBI would develop and maintain a central list of homosexuals against which inquiries could be directed concerning current Government employees or individuals who might apply for Government jobs.[45]

Even though the Sex Deviates Program collected information about homosexuals and Executive Order 10450 banned homosexuals from Federal service, equating this "sexual perversion" with membership in the Communist Party, sabotage, espionage, mental illness, and drug addiction as behaviors constituting dangers to national security, there had never before been a central list at the FBI of American homosexuals. Now there was.[46]

U.S. Civil Service Commission Policies

CSC policy regarding the suitability of homosexuals for Federal employment echoed the findings of the Senate Subcommittee on Investigations. Throughout the 1960's, the application for Federal employment asked all applicants, "Have you ever had, or have you now, homosexual tendencies?"[47] Suitability determinations seemed to hinge on how notorious the CSC believed the homosexual conduct under question was. In 1966, the Chairman of the CSC stated its policy for determining suitability for employment:

> Persons about whom there is evidence that they have engaged in or solicited others to engage in homosexual or sexually perverted acts with them, without evidence of rehabilitation, are not suitable for Federal employment. In acting on such cases the Commission will consider arrest records, court records, or records of conviction for some form of homosexual conduct or sexual perversion; or medical evidence, admissions, or other credible information that the individual has engaged in or solicited others to engage in such acts with him. Evidence showing that a person has homosexual tendencies, standing alone, is insufficient to support a rating of unsuitability on the ground of immoral conduct.[48]

The Chairman also stated that determinations of suitability for employment encompassed the total impact that an applicant had on the job. Among the pertinent considerations regarding the suitability of homosexuals were the revulsion of other employees by homosexual conduct and the resulting disruption of service efficiency; the apprehension of other employees of homosexual advances or assaults; the offense to members of the public who were required to transact business with known "sexual deviates;" the possibility that Government offices would be used to foster homosexual activity, particularly among the youth; and that Government funds or authority would be used to further conduct that was offensive to both the mores and laws of society.[49]

The CSC, the Chairman asserted, applied the standard against criminal, infamous, dishonest, immoral, or notoriously disgraceful conduct uniformly to all suitability investigations. That is, as long as sexual behavior among consenting adults remained truly private, it was not the subject of an inquiry.[50] If an applicant's sexual behavior, be it homosexual or heterosexual, became public by any means, however, an inquiry into suitability could be warranted.[51] If, for example, an applicant for employment proclaimed that he engaged in homosexual conduct, the CSC would be required to find him unsuitable for

Federal employment.[52] "The same would be true of an avowed adulterer, or one who engages in incest, illegal fornication, prostitution, or other sexual acts which are criminal and offensive to our mores and our general sense of propriety."[53] It is ironic that when "once their secretiveness had made homosexuals potential blackmail victims, now their very openness created a danger."[54]

The CSC's Director of Personnel Investigations stated in a 1969 interview that homosexual employees had never been found to be less efficient than their heterosexual counterparts. Their exclusion from employment was because many people continued to regard the presence of homosexual employees in the civil service as repugnant and the CSC disqualified them to retain public confidence. That official predicted, however, that there might come a time when the general public might view homosexuals without repugnance—then, and only then, would the CSC admit homosexuals to the civil service.[55]

Judicial Response

During the 1950's, the courts followed the doctrine that "since Federal employment was not a right, the Government could impose essentially any conditions it chose on that employment."[56] Veterans who happened to be homosexuals had an additional protection in that they could not be dismissed unless their dismissal promoted the efficiency of the service. The courts typically gave great deference to Federal Government agencies in determining exactly what promoted or harmed efficiency.[57]

For example, in *Dew v. Halaby*,[58] the U.S. Court of Appeals for the District of Columbia Circuit upheld the dismissal of a veteran who had worked as an air traffic controller for almost 2 years before the agency discovered evidence of prior specific homosexual acts—in the files of an earlier CIA security clearance investigation. Dew was allowed to resign from the CIA, after which he received an appointment with the Civil Aeronautics Board. The acts for which Dew was dismissed occurred 8 years prior to his removal—when he was 18 or 19 years old.[59]

The Board of Appeals and Review of the CSC concurred with Dew's removal, reasoning that it was in the public interest and promoted the efficiency of the service to remove "employees who have committed such acts and who would not have been selected for appointment had the facts been known prior to appointment."[60] The Appeals Examiner observed that even though it is possible that Dew's "homosexual acts might have no relation to his competence and ability to perform the duties of his position...To require employees to work with persons who have committed acts that are repugnant to the established and accepted standards of decency and morality can only have a disrupting effect upon the morals and efficiency of any organization."[61] The District of Columbia Circuit Court agreed with this assessment.

By 1965, however, at least one court had begun to rethink the latitude that the Government had in proscribing who was and who was not suitable for employment. In *Scott v. Macy*,[62] the District of Columbia Circuit Court found that, "It does not at all follow that because the Constitution does not guarantee a right to public employment, [the Government] may resort to any scheme for keeping people out of such employment...One may not have a constitutional right to go to Baghdad, but the Government may not prohibit one from going there unless by means consonant with due process of law."[63]

Scott had completed a Federal civil service examination and was notified that he had qualified for certain positions subject to further investigation. During this investigation, Scott refused to comment on information in the CSC's possession that indicated he was a homosexual, stating the issue was not pertinent to his job performance. Subsequently, the CSC disqualified Scott for employment for immoral conduct. Scott requested specification of how, when, and where he had conducted himself immorally in order to answer the broad allegation of "immoral conduct." The Board of Appeals and Review of the CSC responded only that "the record disclosed convincing evidence that you have engaged in homosexual conduct, which is considered contrary to generally-recognized and accepted standards of morality."[64]

The District of Columbia Circuit Court ruled that by excluding Scott from the vast field of Federal employment due to an "immoral conduct" charge, the CSC had also stigmatized him in such a way as to jeopardize his ability to find employment elsewhere. The CSC "must at least specify the conduct it finds 'immoral' and state why that conduct related to 'occupational competence or fitness.'"[65] Although the Court ruled for Scott in this instance, the ruling did not preclude the CSC from excluding Scott from eligibility for employment based on some more specific grounds rather than the vague finding of "immoral conduct."[66]

The CSC attempted to do just that—by disqualifying Scott from consideration for employment for his refusal to give testimony in response to the issue of his alleged homosexuality. Scott once again appealed to the District of Columbia Circuit Court, which again ruled in his favor. The majority of the Court was unconvinced that his failure to give testimony—and not his alleged homosexuality—was the reason that the CSC actually disqualified Scott.[67] The Court's decision restored Scott to his original status, as one eligible to be considered for Federal employment.[68]

In its decision, the Court commented on the CSC rules and regulations governing the suitability of homosexuals for public service. The Court found at least three inconsistencies with the CSC's policy that homosexuals were not suitable for Federal employment. First, it appeared to the Court that any homosexual act or solicitation was disqualifying except if one abandoned the practice at some point. Second, in appraising an applicant's conduct, the CSC included a number of pertinent considerations, including "the total impact of the applicant upon the job," which, to the Court, seemed consistent not only with past but also with present and continuing homosexual acts. Finally, the Court noted that the CSC stated that:

> such acts, even though wholly private in nature, are contrary to the criminal laws in virtually all jurisdictions, and that, of necessity therefore, they must be considered to be "immoral conduct." Under this last, it would appear that the only relevant consideration, as contrasted with those which have just been enumerated, is whether an applicant has been or is now committing homosexual acts. The [CSC] then is at some pains to deny that it either does, or can, inquire into private sexual conduct. In its words, "as long as it remains truly private, that is, it remains undisclosed to all but the participants, it is not the subject of an inquiry." But where for some reason it attracts public notice, the [CSC] will ask, and presumably will disqualify, if either there is a refusal to respond or an admission of a homosexual act. Qualification for Federal employment thus appears to turn not upon whether one is a law violator but whether one gets caught.[69]

The CSC policy regarding the suitability of this one type of law breaker seemed to conflict with the way it viewed violations of criminal law in general. That is, to determine suitability, the CSC took into account a variety of matters concerning the law breaking, including the nature and seriousness of the offense, how long ago it occurred, whether it was an isolated or repeat offense, the age of the offender at the time, and the type of position for which the person was applying. "Accordingly, after all the facts [had] been gathered and evaluated, if the applicant [was] considered a good risk offender, his application [would] be rated eligible."[70]

In 1969 the District of Columbia Circuit Court ruled in *Norton v. Macy*[71] that, because it found no reasonable connection between the evidence presented of Norton's alleged homosexual acts and the efficiency of the service, Norton (who was a veteran) had been unlawfully discharged.[72] The mere fact that an employee was a homosexual or had participated in homosexual acts was no longer presumed to automatically harm the efficiency of the service. The Court found that the "notion that it could be an appropriate function of the Federal bureaucracy to enforce the majority's conventional codes of conduct in the private lives of its employees is at war with elementary concepts of liberty, privacy, and diversity."[73] The Court found, however, that there were still a number of ways homosexual conduct might affect the efficiency of the service, including the potential for blackmail, especially where classified information was involved. Moreover, homosexuality "may in some circumstances be evidence of an unstable personality unsuited for certain kinds of work." In addition, according to the Court, if an employee were to make offensive overtures on the job or if his conduct was notorious, the reaction of other employees or the public would be at least broadly relevant to the efficiency of the service.[74]

The decision in *Norton* had little immediate effect on either the CSC or other courts, as both continued to find a routine connection between homosexuality and harm to the efficiency of the service.[75] The CSC complained that the *Norton* decision had placed an "unwarranted burden on the executive branch" by requiring it to prove a connection between employees' off-duty conduct and their Government duties.[76] It was not until 1973 that a class action suit (*Society for Individual Rights, Inc. v. Hampton*)[77] provided the impetus for CSC policies to change. In that case, the U. S. District Court for the Northern District of California followed the holding in *Norton* that employees who were discharged solely because they were homosexuals were discharged improperly.[78] The Court rejected the CSC's view that employing such persons would bring the Government service into "public contempt." The Court held that neither the CSC nor its Board of Appeals and Review had even tried to meet the standard for dismissal set forth in *Norton*—that an employee could only be dismissed for immoral behavior if the behavior actually impaired the efficiency of the service.[79]

There are few reliable figures regarding the number of employees dismissed from, or applicants denied entry to, Federal employment due to their homosexuality beyond those presented in this Section. One estimate places the number of real or suspected homosexuals who lost their civil service jobs in the 1950's between 7,000 and 10,000.[80] It is unlikely that we will ever know how many people were affected by these policies.[81] In *Society for Individual Rights, Inc.*, the CSC was asked to disclose the number of persons who had been discharged annually from the Federal service solely on the grounds of homosexual conduct. The CSC declined to provide that number, claiming that the request was "burdensome and oppressive." The Court interpreted this response to mean that the number of persons discharged on this basis per year was so large that it would be burdensome and oppressive to count them in order to answer what the Court believed to be a proper interrogatory.[82]

Steps Toward Inclusion

The changing posture of the courts concerning the employment of homosexuals in the Federal Government paralleled what the CSC perceived as a gradual change in public attitudes. For example, in a 1971 editorial, *The Washington Post* observed that the barring of homosexuals from sensitive Federal jobs due to the fear of blackmail had often been a pretext for denying them employment. Homosexuals had valuable gifts and insights to bring to Federal employment, the editorial continued, so their persecution was as senseless as it was unjust. Private sexual behavior was none of the Government's business as long as it did not affect an employee's independence and reliability, and, like anyone else, homosexuals had "a right to privacy, a right to opportunity, and a right to serve their country."[83]

Changes in CSC hiring policies regarding sexual orientation that occurred in the 1970's are described below. Subsequent developments in Federal employment policies (also discussed below) included protections afforded employees under the PPPs codified in 1978, a 1998 executive order affirming the Federal policy of not discriminating based on sexual orientation, and recent changes to expand the availability of certain benefits to the same-sex domestic partners and spouses of Federal employees.

Change in Civil Service Policy

As the opinions of the courts began to change in the late 1960's and into the 1970's, the CSC moved to change its policies regarding hiring homosexual individuals. The CSC noted, however, that although public attitudes about what consenting adults did in private were changing, Federal employees did not have the right to debauch their fellow workers, debase their agencies, or bring disgrace to the Government.[84]

In 1971 the CSC observed that the emergence in the law of protections for private conduct protected people who would have been terminated for that same conduct just a few years before. The CSC harkened back to a time when "'living in sin' was widely considered to be exactly that. Employers didn't approve of it at all—it was bad for the organization's reputation—and employees who got caught got out, on request, more or less as a matter of course. Things are different now." The CSC warned, however, that these changes in attitudes or opinions did "not mean that indiscreet, promiscuous, notorious, criminal, or illegal conduct will not support disciplinary actions. It will and does."[85]

It was not until July 1975 that the CSC announced a new approach to determining the suitability of homosexual applicants for Federal employment. The CSC stated that the new guidelines were a significant change from past policies and were a result of court decisions requiring that persons not be disqualified from Federal employment based solely on homosexual conduct. The new guidelines applied the same standards to evaluating sexual conduct, whether heterosexual or homosexual. Although applicants could no longer "be found unsuitable based on unsubstantiated conclusions concerning possible embarrassment for the Federal service, a person may be dismissed or found unsuitable where the evidence exists that sexual conduct affects job fitness."[86]

This change in policy was not absolute, however—the CIA and FBI were exempted from its requirements. Even with this limitation, at least one observer pointed out that the greatest impact of the new guidelines was likely to be the influence they had on other employers, both public and private, across the country.[87]

Prohibited Personnel Practices

On October 13, 1978, President Carter signed into law the Civil Service Reform Act (CSRA) of 1978.[88] The CSRA was the first major overhaul of the Federal personnel system since the creation of the CSC almost 100 years earlier.[89] For the first time, the CSRA codified a set of Merit System Principles (MSPs). Federal personnel management would henceforth be administered in accordance with these MSPs. In addition, the CSRA statutorily defined 11 PPPs that, if not avoided, would undermine the integrity of the merit system.[90]

The Tenth Prohibited Personnel Practice

One PPP enumerated by the CSRA was a prohibition on discriminating against Federal employees or applicants for conduct which was not directly related to their job duties. The tenth PPP states:

> Any employee who has authority to take, direct others to take, recommend, or approve any personnel action, shall not, with respect to such authority... discriminate for or against any employee or applicant for employment on the basis of conduct which does not adversely affect the performance of the employee or applicant or the performance of others; except that nothing in this paragraph shall prohibit an agency from taking into account in determining suitability or fitness any conviction of the employee or applicant for any crime under the laws of any State, of the District of Columbia, or of the United States.[91]

Neither the Administration's original version of the bill nor the Senate's version included this particular PPP—the House of Representatives amended the bill to add it. A conference report that explained how the differing Senate and House versions of the bill were reconciled noted that, as with conduct, convictions that had no bearing on an employee's or applicant's duties or performance could not be the basis for discrimination.[92] The original House version of the tenth PPP defined only certain types of convictions that could be considered in determining suitability or fitness—those for any crime of violence or moral turpitude.[93] Thus, as first drafted, the only convictions that could be taken into account when determining fitness or suitability were those for violent offenses or for a wide range of offenses that might include homosexuality.[94] The language in the bill was changed from "any crime of violence or moral turpitude" to "any crime" by the conference committee.[95]

The CSRA also altered the structure of the administration of Federal civilian personnel management. It abolished the CSC and designated the newly created MSPB as its successor agency. The CSRA transferred most of the original functions of the CSC to the newly created OPM.[96] MSPB retained only those functions of the former CSC relating to hearing and adjudicating employee appeals. The CSRA established an Office of Special Counsel (OSC) within MSPB to operate as its independent investigative and prosecutorial arm. The 1989 Whistleblower Protection Act made OSC an independent agency created to receive, investigate, and prosecute allegations of PPPs.

After passage of the CSRA and the enumeration of the PPPs, OPM Director Alan K. Campbell issued a memorandum which affirmed that Federal employees were prohibited from discriminating based on conduct that did not adversely affect job performance. That 1980 memorandum stated that Federal employees or applicants for employment were protected from actions based on or inquiries into matters such as religious, community, or social affiliations or sexual orientation.[97] The tenth PPP and OPM's interpretation of that PPP to bar sexual orientation discrimination rejected the Subcommittee on

Investigations' earlier conclusion that it was a "false premise that what a Government employee did outside of the office on his own time, particularly if his actions did not involve his fellow employees or his work, was his own business."[98]

An early example of an agency arriving at a similar conclusion for its internal operations occurred at the U.S. Department of Justice in March 1983. At that time, the Assistant Attorney General for Legal Counsel issued a memorandum opinion stating that an Assistant United States Attorney (AUSA) "may not be terminated solely on the basis of his homosexuality, in the absence of a reasonable showing that his homosexuality has adversely affected his job performance."[99] The opinion noted that the authority to remove the AUSA was limited, in part, by the tenth PPP,[100] and that it was doubtful that a nexus could be demonstrated between the AUSA's homosexuality and his job performance because the AUSA had consistently received superior performance ratings.[101]

In 1994 Director James B. King reiterated OPM's policy stance, writing that "OPM has long taken the position that [the tenth PPP] applies directly to discrimination on the basis of sexual orientation."[102] In 1997 OPM again advised agencies that Federal employees were protected against actions taken for non-job related conduct including sexual orientation. OPM recommended that agencies issue a strong management statement that clearly defined this policy, communicate to employees the avenues of redress available if they believed they were subject to discriminatory actions, and review this policy in orientation sessions for new employees.[103]

Federal employees or applicants who believe they have been the subject of a PPP, including sexual orientation discrimination, can file a complaint with OSC. OSC examiners determine whether such complaints contain evidence of a prohibited activity warranting further inquiry. If OSC investigators find sufficient evidence to prove a violation, OSC can seek corrective action, disciplinary action, or both. If OSC is unable to obtain corrective action voluntarily, it may also be obtained by OSC through litigation before MSPB.[104]

In 2013, as a part of its ongoing retrospective analysis of existing regulations, OPM proposed changes to certain nondiscriminatory provisions found in Title 5 of the Code of Federal Regulations.[105] These proposed changes were based partly on OPM's interpretation of 5 U.S.C. § 2302(b)(10) to update and provide consistency among various nondiscrimination provisions. The proposed regulations would include sexual orientation as a nondiscriminatory factor in competitive Federal employment practices, agency merit promotion programs, the selection of Federal employees for training and to receive student loan repayments, and in the operation of merit personnel systems in accordance with the Intergovernmental Personnel Act of 1970. The changes would provide uniform nondiscrimination provisions to the extent permitted by law and, as such, would provide no new avenues of redress for allegations of discrimination.

The Twelfth Prohibited Personnel Practice

Regarding what is today the twelfth PPP, the Senate report for S. 2640, which became the CSRA, stated that the PPP prohibits:[106]

> [A]ny other action which violates any law rule, or regulation implementing, or relating to, the merit system principles constitutes a prohibited personnel practice. This provision was added by the committee in order to make unlawful those actions which are inconsistent with merit system principles, but which do not fall within the [other] categories of personnel practices. Such actions may lead to appropriate discipline. For example, should a supervisor take action against an employee or applicant, without having proper regard for the individual's privacy or constitutional rights, such an action could result in dismissal, fine, reprimand, or other discipline for the supervisor.[107]

OSC has interpreted the twelfth PPP as protecting an employee from adverse actions if such actions are taken because the employee exercised a constitutional right. In *Special Counsel v. Lynn*, OSC sought disciplinary action against two Department of Agriculture officials under 5 U.S.C. § 2302(b)(10) and (12) for proposing and deciding to remove an employee for exercising his First Amendment rights. MSPB ultimately dismissed the complaint at OSC's request because the employing agency implemented discipline on its own, rendering any OSC action duplicative.[108]

The recognition of constitutional rights regarding sexual orientation has evolved since passage of the CSRA and now includes the right to engage in sexual conduct with members of the same sex.[109] Thus, in addition to the tenth PPP, the twelfth PPP may also be pertinent to the rights of lesbian, gay, and bisexual Federal employees.

Executive Order 13087

On May 28, 1998, President Clinton signed Executive Order 13087, *Further Amendment to Executive Order 11478, Equal Employment Opportunity in the Federal Government*, the first executive order to state the policy of non-discrimination based on sexual orientation in Federal employment.[110] By 1998 most individual Federal agencies had issued policies that prohibited such discrimination.[111] The executive order provided a uniform policy by adding sexual orientation to the list of categories for which discrimination in Federal employment was prohibited (e.g., race, color, religion, sex, national origin, disability, and age).[112]

Executive Order 13087 set the stage for positive action by all units of the Federal Government to ensure that the Federal workplace was free from sexual orientation discrimination.[113] It did not, however, establish enforceable rights or remedies for employees who believed they had been discriminated against, such as the ability to proceed before the Equal Employment Opportunity Commission (EEOC). Those rights can only be granted through legislation.[114] To underscore this point, President Clinton issued another executive order in May 2000, amending Executive Order 11478 by stating that no rights or benefits were conferred "enforceable in law or equity against the United States or its representatives."[115] Although some agencies have developed parallel equal employment opportunity (EEO) complaint procedures that allow Federal employees to file EEO complaints based on allegations of sexual orientation discrimination within their agencies,[116] as noted, such complaints cannot proceed on that basis before EEOC.

In June 1999 OPM Director Janice R. Lachance issued guidance to agencies entitled *Addressing Sexual Orientation Discrimination in Federal Civilian Employment—A Guide to Employees' Rights*. This guidance discussed Executive Order 13087 and gave Federal employees information on how they could obtain assistance if they believed they had been discriminated against based on their sexual orientation. The avenues OPM reviewed for such assistance were rooted in 5 U.S.C. § 2302(b)(10) and mirror those discussed in this Section.[117]

Federal Employee Benefit Programs

In 2007 the first Senate-confirmed openly gay United States ambassador resigned his post because he believed the principles of equality that his country promoted abroad were not being implemented at home. The ambassador's partner was not eligible for training that the State Department provided to ambassadorial spouses, the department did not bear the cost of his partner's transportation to his placements abroad, and his partner did not receive other benefits and allowances given to spouses of other ambassadors.[118]

In June 2009, President Obama issued a memorandum intended to address the conditions the ambassador cited as reasons for his resignation and to promote the workplace equality of all LGBT Federal employees.[119] The memorandum announced that certain Federal benefits available to the spouses of heterosexual Federal employees would be extended to the same-sex domestic partners of Federal employees. The memorandum directed the heads of all Federal agencies to conduct a review of other benefits they offered to determine what authority existed to extend them as well.[120]

In addition, the President stated, many "top employers in the private sector already offer benefits to the same-sex partners of their employees; those companies recognize that offering partner benefits helps them compete for and retain the brightest and most talented employees. The Federal Government is at a disadvantage on that score right now, and change is long overdue."[121]

Changes to Federal Employee Benefits

Changes to Federal benefits that occurred in response to the June 2009 memorandum or in response to a second Presidential memorandum the following year[122] include:

- Extending the coverage of child-care subsidies to the children of same-sex domestic partners of lower-income Federal employees.[123]
- Clarifying that a Federal employee's domestic partner and children qualify as family members for access to agency alcohol and drug abuse counseling programs.[124]
- Establishing that an employee's same-sex domestic partner qualifies as a family member for purposes of eligibility for noncompetitive appointment based on overseas employment.[125]
- Amending regulations to add same-sex domestic partners to the class of people for which an insurable interest is presumed to exist.[126]
- Revising regulations to ensure that the same-sex domestic partners of Federal employees and their children have access to evacuation pay and to the separate maintenance allowance for duty at Johnston Island.[127]

- Amending guidance that grants 24 hours of unpaid leave to Federal employees to cover educational activities, routine medical needs, and elderly relatives' health or care needs to include an employee's same-sex domestic partner or the partner's children.[128]
- Modifying the definitions of family member and immediate relative for purposes of the use of sick leave, funeral leave, voluntary leave transfer, voluntary leave bank, and emergency leave transfer.[129]
- Amending the Federal Travel Regulations so that employees and their domestic partners and children can obtain the available benefits including certain travel, relocation, and subsistence payments.[130]
- Expanding the eligibility to apply for long-term care insurance to the same-sex domestic partners of Federal employees and annuitants.[131]

This list is included not only to enumerate the changes that have recently taken place concerning Federal employee benefits but also to give the reader some insight into the daily job-related obstacles that LGBT Federal employees and their partners faced prior to these changes.[132]

In June 2013, two days after the U.S. Supreme Court ruled Section 3 of the Defense of Marriage Act[133] unconstitutional,[134] OPM announced that it would extend certain benefits to Federal employees and annuitants legally married to a spouse of the same sex. Among these benefits were health insurance, life insurance, and retirement benefits. This meant that, for example, the legally married same-sex spouses of Federal employees for the first time were eligible for coverage under the Federal Employees Health Benefits Program, as were the children of same-sex marriages.[135]

In addition to changes in employment policies and the extension of employee benefits, OPM has incorporated sexual orientation in its guidance regarding agency diversity programs. For example, in its November 2011 guidance for the development of agency diversity and inclusion strategic plans, OPM noted that the Federal Government should strive to be the "Nation's model employer by leveraging diversity and fostering inclusion to deliver the best public service."[136] The guidance defined diversity, including sexual orientation, "as a collection of individual attributes that together help agencies pursue organizational objectives efficiently and effectively."[137] Such inclusive policies also can be found in some private sector organizations, as discussed below.

Private Sector Inclusion Policies

A majority of Fortune 500 companies include sexual orientation (88 percent) and gender identity (57 percent) in their non-discrimination policies. In addition, the majority of these companies (62 percent) offer equivalent medical benefits to spouses and partners.[138] Private sector policies that are inclusive of LGBT individuals are indeed important as only 21 States and the District of Columbia have State laws that provide protection from sexual orientation discrimination in employment.[139]

Such policies are responsive to the concerns of many LGBT individuals, who increasingly view equal employment rights as an important priority, as well as to the attitudes of a majority of the general public. According to a 2013 report from the Pew Research Center, when asked to rate the importance of different LGBT-related policy priorities, 57 percent of LGBT survey respondents said equal employment rights should be a top priority. Results of this survey showed that LGBT individuals considered equal employment rights more important than legally-sanctioned same-sex marriage, prevention and treatment of HIV/AIDS, and adoption rights for same-sex couples.[140] According to the Gallup organization, by 2008, support for the principle of equal employment rights of LGBT individuals among the general adult population had held steady at 89 percent for several years.[141]

Besides issues of equality and fairness, there are other reasons that companies provide protections and offer comparable benefits to their LGBT employees. Many top companies believe that embracing diversity in the workplace makes them better employers and better providers of services to their customers.[142]

Inclusive policies may assist in attracting top LGBT talent, but businesses are also concluding that younger employees and applicants who are not members of such groups may care about a business culture that supports women, minorities, and LGBT employees.[143] Not only are some companies trying to appeal to LGBT customers by touting their inclusive policies, they are also cognizant that many heterosexual customers favor strong diversity practices as well.[144] Some companies champion widely diverse work groups because they create more innovative products and bring more ideas and different approaches to the table. Others implement such policies because organizations that include many different perspectives are better able to find more efficient ways to operate and different ways to grow.[145]

THE TENTH PROHIBITED PERSONNEL PRACTICE: EMPLOYEE PERCEPTIONS

Through its Merit Principles Survey (MPS), MSPB has collected data on Federal employee perceptions of discrimination on a variety of bases, including off-duty conduct and sexual orientation.[146] In 2010 the MPS also asked how well Federal employees believe their organizations communicate the prohibition on sexual orientation discrimination in the Federal workplace. This Section summarizes the results of these surveys and explores how Federal employee perceptions of the occurrence of discrimination may be related to how engaged they are in their work. The following Section presents a discussion of LGBT Federal employee attitudes about the workplace.

Discrimination Based on Off-Duty Conduct

In 2010 only two percent of Federal employee respondents to the MPS said that they had been personally affected by discrimination based on off-duty conduct that was entirely unrelated to the job (see **Table 1**).[147] This was a similar percentage to those respondents who perceived that they had been personally affected by other PPPs such as discrimination based on national origin or marital status, being influenced to withdraw from competition for a position, or an agency official practicing nepotism. In addition, six percent of MPS 2010 respondents said that discrimination based on off-duty conduct had occurred in their work unit but that they were not personally affected by it.[148]

Table 1. Percent agreement with the MPS 2010 item: In the past two years, an agency official (e.g. supervisor, manager, senior leader, etc.) in my work unit has discriminated against someone in a personnel action on the basis of off-duty conduct which was entirely unrelated to the job[149]

	Agreement
I was personally affected by this	2%
This has occurred in my work unit, but I was not personally affected by this	6%

Discrimination Based on Sexual Orientation

In response to the MPS in 2005, 2007, and 2010,[150] only about one percent of respondents reported being personally denied a job or job benefit (or otherwise being discriminated against) due to their sexual orientation.[151] About three percent of MPS 2010 respondents perceived that sexual orientation discrimination had occurred in their work unit but such discrimination did not personally affect them. This is a similar percentage of employees who perceived other PPP's had occurred, including discrimination based on national origin and marital status or violations of veteran's preference laws.[152] Given the history of sexual orientation discrimination in Federal employment described earlier in this report, such low reported perceptions of continuing discrimination are indeed welcome.

This low rate of perceived sexual orientation discrimination is consistent with the results of OPM's 2012 FEVS. Although the FEVS did not ask directly about respondent experiences with discrimination, it asked whether respondents agreed that PPPs are not tolerated. A similar percentage of heterosexual employees and LGBT employees agreed with this statement (see **Table 2**). Leaving aside a discussion of the broader implications of only about two-thirds of Federal employees agreeing with this statement, it would appear that the experiences of heterosexual and LGBT employees concerning PPPs are similar. (More results from the 2012 FEVS are presented in the next Section.)

Table 2. Percent agreement with the FEVS 2012 item: Prohibited Personnel Practices (for example, illegally discriminating for or against any employee/applicant, obstructing a person's right to compete for employment, knowingly violating veterans' preference requirements) are not tolerated[153]

	Agreement
Heterosexual employees	67%
LGBT employees	64%

Data regarding the incidence of perceived sexual orientation discrimination among Federal employees are not easily comparable to data in other employment sectors. This is because the data discussed in this section either refer to perceptions of all Federal employees regarding sexual orientation discrimination, or the data refer to LGBT Federal employee perceptions regarding the occurrence of the broader PPPs. We have no data on the specific question of whether LGBT Federal employees believe they have been the victims of sexual orientation discrimination.

Other surveys based in other employment sectors have asked lesbian, gay, and bisexual (LGB) individuals about their experience with job discrimination. For example, one 2009 study based on a national probability sample found 10 percent of LGB individuals reported being discriminated against due to their perceived sexual orientation.[154] In addition, a 2013 national survey found that 26 percent of gay men, 23 percent of lesbians, and 15 percent of bisexuals believed they had been treated unfairly by an employer because they were or were perceived to be lesbian, gay, or bisexual.[155]

Relationship to Employee Engagement

Previous MSPB research found a relationship between the engagement level of Federal employees and certain desirable agency outcomes. That research defined employee engagement as a heightened connection between employees and their work, their organization, or the people they work for or with. We found that in Federal agencies where more employees were engaged, better program results were produced, employees used less sick leave, fewer employees filed EEO complaints, and there were lower rates of work-related injury or illness.[156]

There are many factors from one's intrinsic motivation to the culture of one's organization that may affect the engagement level of an employee. We expected employees who perceived that they have been the victims of outright discrimination or any other PPP to be less engaged in their work than those who did not harbor those perceptions. Further MSPB examination of the MPS 2010 results confirmed this expectation and showed that the effects were not limited to employees who perceived that they had been the specific targets of such practices. Employees who believed these practices were occurring in the work unit but who were not directly affected were also typically less engaged than other employees.[157]

As with PPPs in general, survey respondents who believed they were personally affected by sexual orientation discrimination were far less engaged than respondents who did not believe sexual orientation discrimination had occurred in their work unit (see **Table 3**). Survey respondents who were not personally affected by sexual orientation discrimination but believed it had happened in their work unit were also less engaged.

Table 3. Level of employee engagement based on responses to the MPS 2010 item: In the past two years, an agency official (e.g. supervisor, manager, senior leader, etc.) in my work unit has discriminated in favor or against someone in a personnel action based upon sexual orientation

	Engaged	*Not engaged*
I was personally affected by this	12%	64%
This has occurred in my work unit but I was not personally affected by this	13%	46%
This has not occurred in my work unit	53%	9%

Remaining respondents fell into the "somewhat engaged" category.

PPPs should be avoided because to commit one is to violate the law, and the offender may be subject to adverse action, up to and including removal from the Federal service.[158] In noting that employees who do not perceive PPPs are occurring are far more engaged, however, we present a solid business case for avoiding PPPs. As with the perception of any PPP, the negative effects of sexual orientation discrimination spread wider than the individual directly affected— other employees in the work unit see what is happening and their level of engagement may decrease. When levels of employee engagement drop, organizational results and other positive outcomes are likely to suffer.

Communicating the Policy of Non-Discrimination

The Notification and Federal Employee Antidiscrimination and Retaliation Act

In 2002 Congress enacted the Notification and Federal Employee Antidiscrimination and Retaliation Act,[159] which requires agencies to provide notification to Federal employees of their rights and protections regarding discrimination and retaliation.[160] OPM's regulations that implemented this act provided sample language for agencies to use for this notification, including:

> A Federal agency cannot discriminate against an employee or applicant with respect to the terms, conditions or privileges of employment on the basis of race, color, religion, sex, national origin, age, disability, marital status or political affiliation...If you believe that you have been the victim of unlawful discrimination on the basis of race,

color, religion, sex, national origin or disability, you must contact an...EEO counselor within 45 calendar days[.][161]

When the OPM regulations were proposed, several commenters suggested that the regulations be expanded to cover the tenth PPP and Executive Order 13087, which would include sexual orientation discrimination as a form of prohibited discrimination. OPM concluded, however:

> [T]he No FEAR Act does not directly refer to 5 U.S.C. 2302(b)(10) as a law covered by the Act or refer to Executive Order 13087 (or 11478) as being covered by the Act. The regulations address those matters directly identified in the No FEAR Act. Therefore, the suggestion is not adopted.[162]

Congressional action to specifically prohibit sexual orientation discrimination in Federal employment would undoubtedly provide greater visibility to this issue.

Absent this visibility, Federal agencies may have to play a greater role in communicating the requirements of Executive Order 13087 than they may have to play regarding other types of discrimination that are specifically prohibited by legislation. The notification that Federal agencies are required to provide to their employees by the No FEAR Act could have been a method to provide such guidance regarding sexual orientation discrimination.

Agency Communication

Although some agencies may include sexual orientation as part of the required No FEAR Act training, we wanted to know how effective agencies have been in communicating to employees the policy of non-discrimination based on sexual orientation in the Federal workplace. To this end, the MPS 2010 asked Federal employees whether their organization has made it clear that it prohibits sexual orientation discrimination. Among nonsupervisory employees, 68 percent agreed that their organizations had made this policy clear, while 81 percent of supervisors agreed. Among all employees, agreement with this statement varied across agencies from 58 percent to 82 percent (see **Table 4**).

Table 4. Percent agreement with the MPS 2010 item: My organization has made it clear that it prohibits discrimination based on a person's sexual orientation

	Agreement
Supervisors	81%
Non-supervisors	68%
Agency with most agreement	82%
Agency with least agreement	58%

Typically, 81 percent of supervisors agreeing with a positive statement would seem like a good result for most types of survey questions. In this case, however, it means that nearly one in every five supervisors—who make important decisions regarding their employees every day— did not report that their organizations have made it clear that supervisors are prohibited from engaging in sexual orientation discrimination.

Unfortunately, because we have no data on the extent to which survey respondents have been notified of the prohibition on other forms of discrimination, we cannot place these survey results into a proper context.[163] If, however, survey results showed that about one-fifth of Federal supervisors (and over one-third of some agency workforces) did not agree that their organizations have made it clear that they prohibit discrimination on any other another basis (sex, religion, or disability, for example), it would rightly raise concern.

LGBT Employee 2012 FEVS Results

This Section presents results from OPM's 2012 FEVS. The FEVS is a tool used by OPM and Federal agencies to provide annual snapshots of employees' perceptions of whether characteristics of successful organizations are present in their organizations. After a pilot study in 2011, the full 2012 FEVS asked respondents for the first time to self-identify as heterosexual or straight, as lesbian or gay, as bisexual, as transgender, or to indicate that they preferred not to self-identify their sexual orientation.[164]

Over 687,000 Federal employees from 82 agencies responded to the 2012 FEVS, for a response rate of 46 percent.[165] For the current study, OPM made data from the 40 largest agencies available for review. To ensure the confidentiality of respondents from smaller agencies, OPM consolidated respondent data from the remaining 42 agencies into a single small agency category.[166] Unless otherwise indicated, the data presented in this Section represent MSPB analysis of weighted results of the 2012 FEVS.[167]

Results of the 2012 FEVS form the first large-scale data set that exists regarding the LGBT Federal workforce. Therefore, we present the demographic data made available for review below to give an initial picture of some of the characteristics of the LGBT portion of the Federal workforce.[168] After this demographic data is presented, we discuss LGBT Federal employee perceptions of the workplace.

LGBT Employee Demographics

As shown in **Table 5**, about two percent of the respondents to the 2012 FEVS self-identified as LGBT. This means the 2012 FEVS measured the attitudes of over 13,500 Federal employees who self-identified as LGBT.[169] By comparison, other studies have estimated the percentage of adults in the United States who identify as LGBT at between three and four percent of the adult population.[170]

Table 5. FEVS LGBT respondent proportion of various demographic categories[171]

Respondents	Heterosexual or straight	LGBT	I prefer not to say
All*	87.0%	2.2%	10.8%
By gender:			
Male	88.2%	2.3%	9.5%
Female	85.7%	2.2%	12.1%
By supervisory status:			
Supervisory**	87.1%	2.4%	10.5%
Non-supervisory***	87.0%	2.2%	10.8%
By age group:			
39 and younger	88.5%	2.9%	8.6%
40-49	87.4%	2.5%	10.0%
50 and older	86.5%	1.7%	11.7%

* 2012 Federal Employee Viewpoint Survey Results—Governmentwide Management Report, op. cit., p. 28.

** Includes supervisors, managers, and executives.

*** Includes non-supervisors and team leaders.

About 11 percent of 2012 FEVS respondents declined to identify their sexual orientation. Among agency workforces, the percentage that declined to identify their sexual orientation ranged from 8 percent to 18 percent.[172] Employees may have a number of reasons for not sharing this information, ranging from belief that it is no one's business to fear that the information will not be kept confidential. Employees who believe their workplace is less than safe or supportive may be unwilling to share this information. Our analysis of the 2012 FEVS results showed that the greatest determinant in whether respondents disclosed their sexual orientation was related to their global satisfaction. Respondents were more receptive to disclosing their sexual orientation if they were highly satisfied with their work, their workplace, and their organizational leadership.

One previous nationally representative survey of the workplace attitudes of LGBT employees found that 72 percent of those employees would self-disclose their sexual orientation or gender identity along with other demographic information in an anonymous human resources survey. Unfortunately, we do not know what percentage of LGBT Federal employees declined to self-identify their sexual orientation on the 2012 FEVS. According to the same national survey, two-thirds of LGBT employees said one reason they are not open about their sexual orientation to everyone at work is because they believe "it's nobody's business." That survey also found that this belief was closely tied to a negative workplace climate—employees who believed their sexual orientation was nobody's business were most likely to feel unaccepted by coworkers.[173]

Although the differences in percentages were small, it appears that younger employees were more willing to disclose their sexual orientation on the 2012 FEVS than were older employees. As can be seen in **Table 5,** about 9 percent of respondents age 39 and younger, as opposed to about 12 percent of respondents age 50 and older, declined to identify their sexual orientation.

The two percent figure who self-identified as LGBT was fairly stable across the other 2012 FEVS demographic items that OPM provided for review. For example, (as shown in **Table 5**) two to three percent of both genders, both supervisory statuses, and all age groups self-identified as LGBT. We noted in the previous Section that similar percentages of 2012 FEVS heterosexual respondents and LGBT respondents agreed that PPPs are not tolerated. That LGBT employees appear to be represented in the supervisory, managerial, and executive ranks in the same proportion as they are in the overall workforce may be another indication that discrimination against LGBT individuals in Federal employment is being remedied.

LGBT Employee Perceptions of the Federal Workplace

OPM has previously published data on LGBT Federal employee perceptions of the workplace through a number of indices OPM tracks as a part of the FEVS process. These findings are summarized below as are the findings from our agency-based analysis of the 2012 FEVS results.

2012 FEVS Indices

The 2012 FEVS included six indices that provide a consistent method for Federal agencies to assess different facets of their workforces. Four of these indices provide metrics for assessing agency management of human capital as provided for by the Human Capital Assessment and Accountability Framework (HCAAF).[174] These four indices are: Leadership and Knowledge Management, Results-Oriented Performance Culture, Talent Management, and Job Satisfaction. The remaining two FEVS indices are Global Satisfaction (a combination of employees' satisfaction with their job, their pay, and their organization, and their willingness to recommend their organization as a good place to work) and Employee Engagement (which consists of three additional indices: Leaders Lead, Supervisors, and Intrinsic Work Experiences).[175] This measure of employee engagement was developed by OPM through the FEVS process and is different than MSPB's measure of employee engagement discussed earlier in this report.

The scores for each of these indices for LGBT and non-LGBT employees are listed in **Table 6**. OPM calculated these scores by averaging the percent positive responses on the survey items within each index.[176] As reported by OPM, employees who self-identified as LGBT responded less positively than non-LGBT employees across all indices.

The differences between the FEVS index scores for LGBT and non-LGBT respondents only range between four and six percentage points. Although these differences are small, those small differences become more important because there is a pattern of less positive LGBT responses across all of the indices. The indices listed in **Table 6** include 47 separate questions from the 2012 FEVS. The pattern of less positive LGBT responses across the indices also holds for those underlying questions—LGBT respondents had less positive attitudes on each of those 47 questions. The difference in LGBT and non-LGBT positive responses to those questions ranged from one to eight percentage points, with an average difference of five percentage points.[178]

Table 6. 2012 FEVS indices scores for self-identified LGBT and non-LGBT respondents[177]

	Average of percent positive responses	
Index	LGBT	Not LGBT
Human Capital Assessment and Accountability Framework		
Leadership and Knowledge Management	56	62
Results-Oriented Performance Culture	50	54
Talent Management	55	60
Job Satisfaction	62	67
Employee Engagement	62	67
Leaders Lead	50	56
Supervisors	68	72
Intrinsic Work Experiences	67	72
Global Satisfaction	59	65

Agency Differences

We examined the generally less positive perceptions of the LGBT Federal workforce described in the previous section to see if they varied depending on the employing agency. Our examination of the 2012 FEVS results revealed that, in some agencies, there was a small but statistically significant relationship between survey responses on the LGBT item and how strongly respondents endorsed other items on the survey. For the questions for which this relationship existed, LGBT employee attitudes were less positive than heterosexual employee attitudes. In other agencies, status on the LGBT item had no effect on how strongly (or weakly) LGBT employees endorsed other survey items.

Our analysis focused on 3 clusters of questions from the 2012 FEVS (16 questions in all) that we grouped into the following categories: Leadership, Work Environment, and Training.[179] The results of our analysis are discussed in the remainder of this section and show that, in some agencies for these survey items, LGBT perceptions are generally less positive than their heterosexual colleagues while in other agencies LGBT employee perceptions of these three workplace components are very similar to the perceptions of heterosexual employees.[180]

Leadership

Table 7 lists the questions included in the Leadership Cluster. The Leadership questions involve how employees view the effectiveness of the management above the level of their immediate supervisor. Effective leaders set a vision for the organization, empower employees to make the vision a reality, respond to employee concerns, and ultimately play a large role in how satisfied employees are with the organization.

Table 7. 2012 FEVS Leadership Cluster questions

30.	Employees have a feeling of personal empowerment with respect to work processes.
41.	I believe the results of this survey will be used to make my agency a better place to work.
57.	Managers review and evaluate the organization's progress toward meeting its goals andobjectives.
58.	Managers promote communication among different work units (for example, aboutprojects, goals, needed resources).
59.	Managers support collaboration across work units to accomplish work objectives.
60.	Overall, how good a job do you feel is being done by the manager directly above yourimmediate supervisor/team leader?
61.	I have a high level of respect for my organization's senior leaders.
62.	Senior leaders demonstrate support for Work/Life programs.
71.	Considering everything, how satisfied are you with your organization?

As can be seen in **Figure 2**, there were differences in perception between LGBT and heterosexual employees regarding leadership within some agencies. There were other agencies, however, where LGBT employee and heterosexual employee attitudes about leadership were very similar. For example, **Figure 3** shows that the attitudes among LGBT and heterosexual employees in the National Aeronautics and Space Administration (NASA), concerning the questions within the Leadership Cluster, were almost identical.

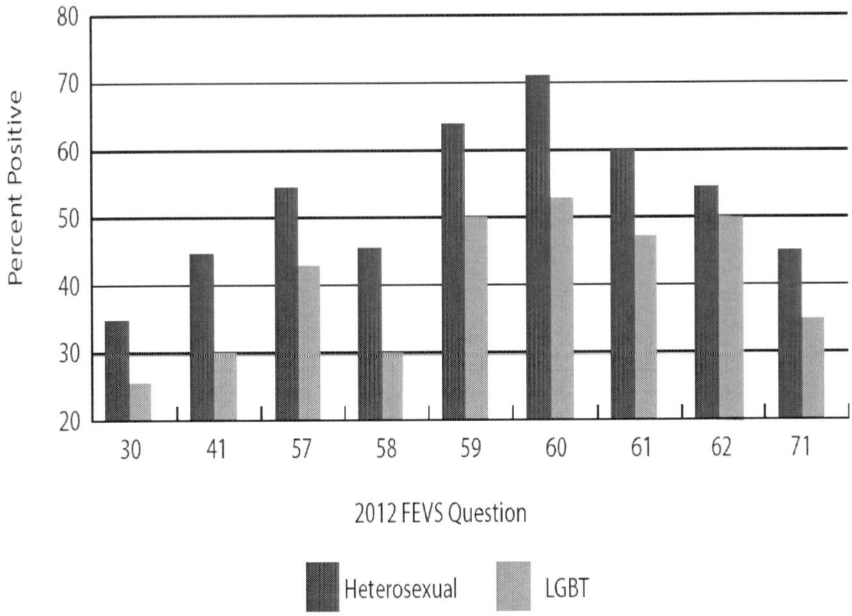

Figure 2. Percent positive responses to Leadership Cluster questions among heterosexual and LGBT respondents within selected agencies with a significant LGBT effect for each question.[181]

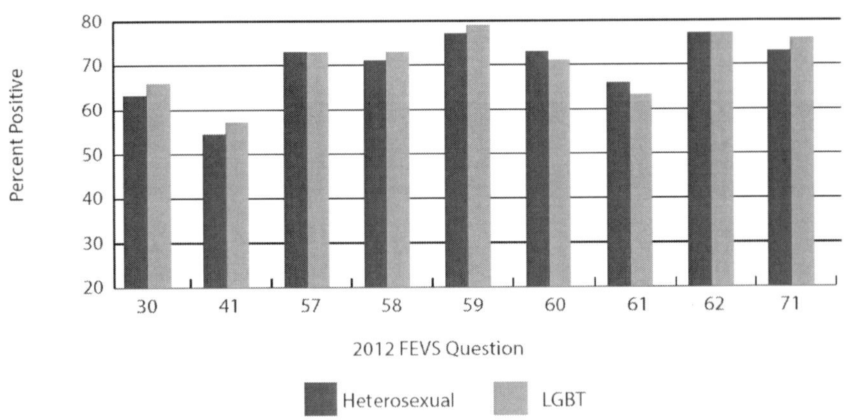

Figure 3. Percent positive responses to Leadership Cluster questions among heterosexual and LGBT respondents in NASA.

Work Environment

Table 8 lists the questions included in the Work Environment Cluster. The Work Environment Cluster questions involve how employees perceive the physical conditions in which they work, whether they are prepared for security threats, and whether the work environment promotes diversity and values reports of wrongdoing.

Table 8. 2012 FEVS Work Environment Cluster questions

14.	Physical conditions (for example, noise level, temperature, lighting, cleanliness in the workplace) allow employees to perform their jobs well.
17.	I can disclose a suspected violation of any law, rule or regulation without fear of reprisal.
34.	Policies and programs promote diversity in the workplace (for example, recruiting minorities and women, training in awareness of diversity issues,mentoring).
36.	My organization has prepared employees for potential security threats.

As can be seen in **Figure 4**, there were differences in perception between LGBT and heterosexual employees regarding the work environment within some agencies. There were other agencies, however, where LGBT employee and heterosexual employee attitudes about the work environment were very similar. For example, **Figure 5** shows that the attitudes among LGBT and heterosexual employees in the General Services Administration (GSA), concerning the questions within the Work Environment Cluster, were almost identical.

Training

Table 9 lists the questions included in the Training Cluster. Beyond satisfaction with training and whether employees' training needs are assessed, the Training Cluster includes whether employees believe they have enough information to do their job well.

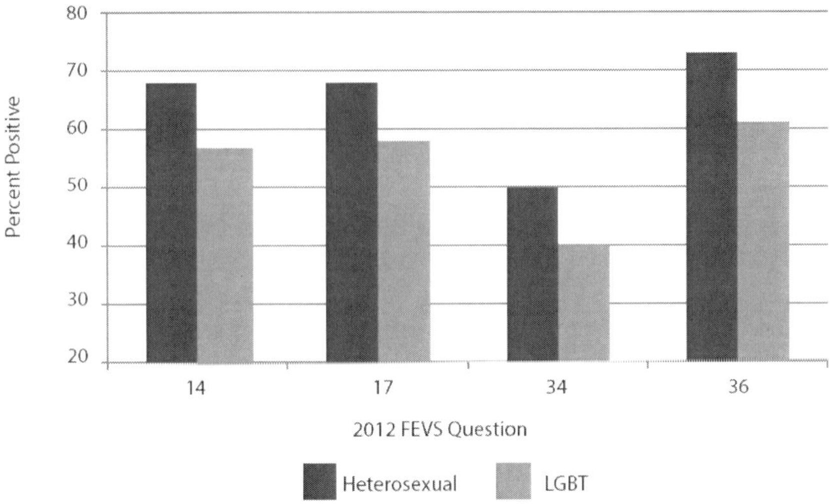

Figure 4. Percent positive responses to Work Environment Cluster questions among heterosexual and LGBT respondents within selected agencies with a significant LGBT effect for each question.[182]

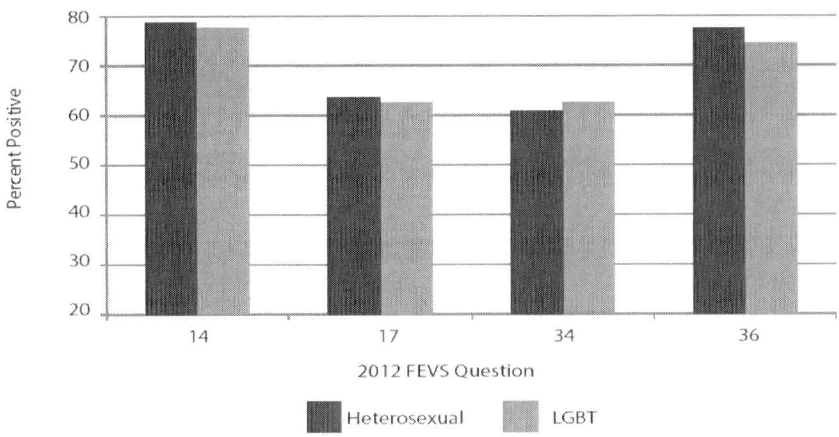

Figure 5. Percent positive responses to Work Environment Cluster questions among heterosexual and LGBT respondents in GSA.

Table 9. 2012 FEVS Training Cluster question

2.	I have enough information to do my job well.
18.	My training needs are assessed.
68.	How satisfied are you with the training you receive for your present job?

As with our previous two clusters, there were differences in perception between LGBT and heterosexual employees regarding training within some agencies (see **Figure 6**). Again, we observe that there were some agencies where LGBT employee and heterosexual employee attitudes about training were very similar. For example, **Figure 7** shows the percentage of positive attitudes of LGBT and heterosexual employees in the Department of Health and Human Services (HHS) for the questions in the Training Cluster. Regarding these questions, attitudes among these two groups of employees within HHS were almost identical.

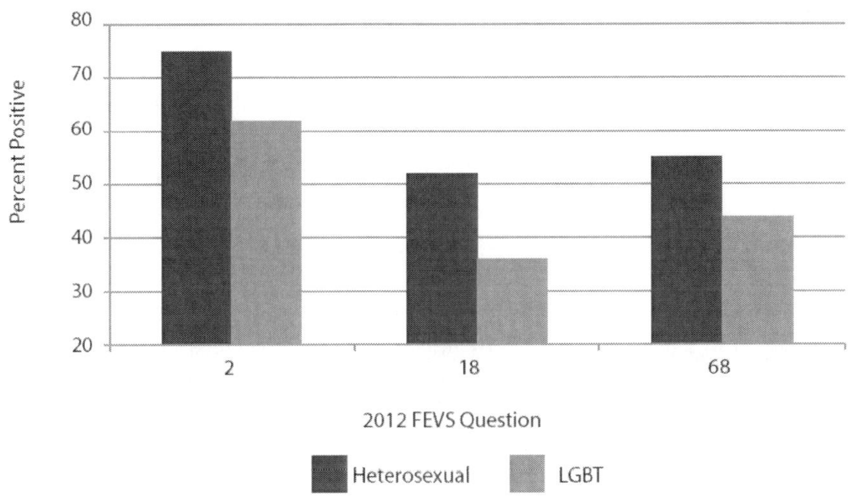

Figure 6. Percent positive responses to Training Cluster questions among heterosexual and LGBT respondents within selected agencies with a significant LGBT effect for each question.[183]

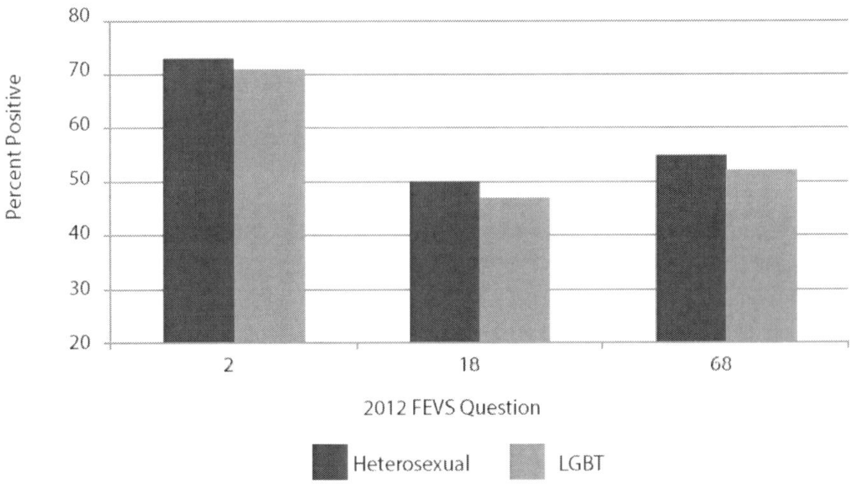

Figure 7. Percent positive responses to Training Cluster questions among heterosexual and LGBT respondents in HHS.

Research has identified some factors that could cause LGBT employees to view their workplace less positively than other individuals. Although neither previous MSPB surveys nor the FEVS have asked if LGBT respondents have self-disclosed their sexual orientation at work, one nationally representative survey found that 51 percent of LGBT workers hide their LGBT identity from most people at work.[184] The consequences of hiding one's LGBT identity may include having to lie daily about one's personal life and being unable to participate honestly in everyday conversations at work which may hinder trust and cohesion with one's coworkers and superiors.[185] Whether due to the workplace climate or other reasons, the belief that one must conceal such an integral part of oneself in the workplace may reduce employees' ability to perform their best, as well as their attitudes about the workplace (as measured by instruments such as the FEVS).[186]

A number of other factors could contribute to these less positive attitudes as well. In addition to perceiving outright discrimination, if LGBT employees perceive non-inclusiveness either in the policies of their managers or the attitudes of their coworkers, we would expect them to harbor less positive attitudes about the workplace. It is also understandable for Federal employees to have less positive attitudes if they perceive employment protections as confusing or inadequate, or they believe employee benefits are administered inequitably.

Future researchers or agencies themselves may undertake studies to determine why differences exist in some agencies for some FEVS questions. This level of detailed inquiry was beyond the scope of the current study. We note, however, that individual characteristics of agencies such as organizational culture and management practices can contribute to any employee's positive or negative perceptions about the workplace. It is safe to say that these same characteristics play a part in LGBT employee perceptions of the workplace as well.

THE CURRENT STATE OF PROTECTION FROM SEXUAL ORIENTATION DISCRIMINATION

In completing this study we encountered a number of peculiarities in how Federal employment policy regarding sexual orientation discrimination evolved. In 2005 legislation was introduced in the House of Representatives to dispel any confusion that may have existed regarding the protections from sexual orientation discrimination in the Federal workplace—so we are not alone in noting the ambiguity that surrounds this topic.[187] We briefly summarize below the current state of protection from sexual orientation discrimination in the Federal workplace.

Federal Government Policy

It is the policy of the Federal Government that sexual orientation discrimination is prohibited in Federal employment. As significant a step as the signing of Executive Order 13087 was in stating the policy of non-discrimination based on sexual orientation, however, it was just that—a policy statement. It provided for no enforceable rights for employees who believe they are victims of sexual orientation discrimination. Employees have no individual right of action to independently seek review from the EEOC for claims of sexual orientation discrimination.[188]

Prohibited Personnel Practices

The tenth PPP prohibits discriminating based on conduct that does not adversely affect an employee's performance. Since 1980 OPM has interpreted this prohibition to include sexual orientation discrimination. Therefore, Federal employees are free to petition OSC if they believe they have been discriminated against on this basis. If OSC finds enough evidence of wrongdoing it may petition the agency in question for corrective action.

Federal employees may raise the tenth PPP as an affirmative defense in an otherwise appealable action before MSPB. It is important to remember, however, that although OSC will accept a complaint alleging discrimination based on sexual orientation under the tenth PPP, neither MSPB nor the courts have resolved whether sexual orientation alone is enough to prevail under 5 U.S.C. § 2302(b)(10).[189]

Differing Interpretations

In 2004 the Special Counsel determined that the protections found at 5 U.S.C. § 2302(b)(10) did *not* extend to sexual orientation discrimination. At that time, OSC was accepting claims based on sexual orientation discrimination but was evaluating them to see if some other standard applied.[190] The White House subsequently issued a statement affirming that President Bush believed "that no Federal employee should be subject to unlawful discrimination, and Federal agencies will fully enforce the law against discrimination, including discrimination based on sexual orientation."[191] It was the confusion raised by these events that the bill introduced in the House of Representatives in 2005 (discussed in the introduction to this Section) was meant to dispel.[192]

Senator Daniel K. Akaka observed during a Senate committee hearing in 2009 that OSC had recently updated its website to once again explain that sexual orientation discrimination *was* actually a PPP subject to investigation by OSC. According to Senator Akaka, Federal employees had been provided inaccurate and inconsistent guidance on this issue.[193]

Agency Policies

Some agencies have developed procedures that parallel agency EEO complaint processes to hear employee complaints of sexual orientation discrimination.[194] These procedures undoubtedly provide a valuable avenue for the airing and resolution of such complaints. The existence of these parallel procedures, however, may lead to confusion. For example, employees may assume that the basis for their sexual orientation discrimination complaint is rooted in statute similar to other matters brought into the agency EEO process. Employees may also assume that the avenues of redress available for allegations of sexual orientation discrimination outside of agency processes are similar to those available to employees alleging discrimination on other bases. Both of these assumptions are false.

No FEAR Act

In 2002 Congress enacted the No FEAR Act, which requires agencies to notify Federal employees of their rights and protections regarding discrimination and retaliation. The No FEAR Act did not, however, require for employees to be notified of the protections that exist from sexual orientation discrimination, and consequently neither did OPM's implementing regulations.

Court and EEOC Decisions

The Supreme Court has held that whether a victim of discrimination is gay or bisexual does not preclude a claim under Title VII of the Civil Rights Act of 1964. In two separate cases, the court ruled that Title VII claims can proceed if lesbian, gay, or bisexual individuals can demonstrate that they were the victims of unlawful sex discrimination in the form of sexual harassment or gender stereotyping. Therefore, these individuals may be protected under Title VII if they are discriminated against based on sex, but they are not protected under current law if they claim discrimination based on sexual orientation.[195]

EEOC has also ruled that lesbian, gay, and bisexual individuals may also experience sex discrimination.[196] For example, it has ruled that an ongoing pattern of referring to an individual as "gay" can be pervasive enough to rise to the level of sexual harassment[197] and that sex discrimination may include adverse actions taken because of an individual's failure to conform to sex-stereotypes.[198]

RECOMMENDATIONS

Given the history of sexual orientation discrimination in Federal employment, it is encouraging that so few Federal employees perceive that such discrimination occurs today. More research will be needed to determine the more relevant point—how many LGB employees believe such discrimination occurs (as well as how many transgender Federal employees believe gender identity discrimination occurs). It is also encouraging that LGBT Federal employees appear to be represented among the supervisory and managerial cadre at a rate comparable to their representation in non-supervisory positions. We note, however, that there are issues inherent in the existing protections from sexual orientation discrimination as well as in the communication of those protections.

The recent nominees to lead the agencies that deal with Federal employment policy and the prosecution of allegations of PPPs—OPM and OSC—have typically been asked as part of the Senatorial confirmation process whether they agree with the interpretation that the tenth PPP bars sexual orientation discrimination.[199] This practice illustrates the fundamental limitation of current policy—the existence and enforcement of protections against sexual orientation discrimination in Federal employment depend on interpretation. Any ambiguity in the longstanding policy prohibiting sexual orientation discrimination would be resolved by legislation making that prohibition explicit. Such legislation could grant Federal employees who allege they are victims of sexual orientation discrimination access to the same remedies as those who allege discrimination on other bases.

MSPB recommends the following actions be taken to further the inclusion of LGBT employees in the Federal workplace:

Federal Agencies Should:

- As required by OPM's *Guidance for Agency-Specific Diversity and Inclusion Strategic Plans*, review their management programs, policies, and procedures to ensure they are inclusive, transparent, and fair to all employees—and that they are perceived as such by employees. OPM's guidance provides specific steps that agencies may take to complete this analysis.[200]

- Support employee affinity groups focused on LGBT issues. In addition to signaling to all employees that the workplace is open and inclusive, agency sponsored LGBT affinity groups may be consulted when management policies are developed or changed. Such groups can also assist with recruitment efforts, mentoring, and other retention-focused activities.[201]
- Remain vigilant against PPPs and other activities including instances of sexual orientation discrimination that may undermine the actual or perceived integrity of agency human resources programs. Although the percentage of employees reporting violations of the MSPs or instances of PPPs are low, Federal agencies should seek to further reduce the incidence of illegal behaviors through education, appropriate redress mechanisms, and accountability for employees who abuse personnel authorities, commit PPPs, or tolerate such actions.[202]
- Provide training for (and on-going communication to) all employees regarding the prohibition on discriminating based on an employee's or an applicant's sexual orientation. Such training could be part of agency general diversity and inclusion instruction. The procedures for filing a complaint if employees believe they have been discriminated against on this basis should be included in agency training and communication efforts. In addition, these topics should be addressed as part of the training provided to new supervisors.
- Monitor the attitudes and perceptions of LGBT employees through FEVS data, other survey instruments, or employee focus groups to ascertain whether agency diversity and inclusion efforts are successful.

The Office of Personnel Management Should:

- Continue to include an item regarding sexual orientation and gender identity in future Federal Employee Viewpoint Surveys. Such data can assist agencies in crafting more inclusive management policies and can be used to benchmark employee attitudes across agencies.
- Consider adding an item to the FEVS regarding employee perceptions of whether they have been discriminated against and, if so, on what basis they believe that discrimination occurred. The results of this

survey item will fill an important gap in our understanding of LGBT issues across the civilian service.

Managers and Supervisors Should:

- Foster an inclusive work environment that is open to and accepting of all employees by managing in accordance with the MSPs while avoiding PPPs. The extent to which managers and supervisors discharge their authority in accordance with these ideals can influence the extent to which LGBT employees believe they are accepted in the workplace.[203]

Federal Employees Should:

- Make the effort to understand individual differences and work effectively with colleagues regardless of those differences. In most organizations, an employee who is merely tolerated, or left to his or her own, is unlikely to remain, much less thrive. The benefits of diversity—bringing a range of perspectives to bear on agency problems, courses of action, and how those actions may be perceived— can only be realized when employees work proactively to attain those benefits.[204]
  It can be challenging to work with individuals whose interests, values, or beliefs differ from our own. We acknowledge these challenges can be uncomfortable for employees. It is imperative, however, that personal discomfort—with the differences themselves, or with the effort needed to bridge them—not be allowed to interfere with the sharing of work-related information and the accomplishment of work unit and agency goals.[205]

Future Researchers Should:

- Review the protections afforded transgender Federal employees, their attitudes toward those protections, and their perceptions of the work environment. These steps will help determine what additional actions, if any, should be taken to make the Federal workplace more inclusive of these individuals.

These recommendations are intended to promote the management of civilian Federal employees in accordance with the MSPs while being free from PPPs. The MSPs state that all employees and applicants for Federal employment should receive fair and equitable treatment with proper regard for their privacy and constitutional rights, and should be protected against arbitrary action and personal favoritism.[206] They also require that the Federal Government's recruitment policies strive for a workforce that is representative of all segments of society.[207] A commitment to equal opportunity, diversity, and inclusion is critical to achieving this goal.

Not only is attaining a diverse, qualified workforce one of the cornerstones of the merit-based civil service, as "the nation's largest employer, the Federal Government has a special obligation to lead by example."[208]

APPENDIX: METHODS

We used a number of processes to determine if the way people responded to the 2012 FEVS LGBT item affected the way they responded to other FEVS questions, and whether differences between LGBT and non-LGBT respondents were statistically significant within and between agencies. If being LGBT made no significant difference to a question's positivity or negativity, we concluded that the question did not vary by sexual orientation. If, however, a question's answer depended on whether one was LGBT, heterosexual, or declined to self-identify, then we concluded that sentiments expressed on this question varied significantly based on one's sexual orientation. In this way, we measured the effect of being LGBT on responses to questions and clusters of questions and could compare these effects across agencies.

We compiled a list of FEVS questions where the LGBT effect was statistically significant for any agency. We found 22 FEVS questions that showed a small but statistically significant LGBT effect for at least 16 different agencies. In our estimation, if an FEVS question showed a statistically significant LGBT effect in more than 15 agencies, the effect had occurred in enough agencies to warrant discussion in the report—some of these items were statistically significant in as many as 23 agencies. For ease of discussion, we classified these 22 questions into various groups that we had earlier identified through a factor analysis, also based on the FEVS LGBT question.

Factor analysis is commonly used to determine how many latent variables underlie a set of questions such as the responses to the 2012 FEVS. It is also used to explain the variation among many original variables (all of the items in the 2012 FEVS, for example) using fewer newly created variables (the factors). In this way, the factor analysis process condenses large numbers of questions into a smaller, more manageable set of factors. Factor analysis is also used to define the substantive content or meaning of each of the factors or latent variables.[209]

We determined that, if 3 or more of these 22 questions fell into a single factor, the factor would be further analyzed and discussed in the report. Of these 22 questions, 16 fell into 3 of our factors—Leadership (9 questions), Work Environment (4 questions), and Training (3 questions). These three factors are discussed in the text of the report. The remaining six FEVS questions were spread across five other factors, meaning each of those factors had less than our three-question threshold for being further analyzed or discussed in the report.

Analyses of survey results that are presented in this report exclude "don't know/not applicable" responses to focus on those who reported an opinion in response to a survey question.

All data that are presented in this report have been rounded either to the nearest percentage or to the nearest tenth of a percentage. This may cause some within-item data to appear not to total 100 percent.

In addition to the sources cited in the text of the report, our study was informed by OPM responses to a MSPB questionnaire regarding the current status and possible future of employment protections based on sexual orientation in the Federal workplace. We also sought input from knowledgeable individuals within the Federal EEO community and academia.

End Notes

[1] "Transgender" is an umbrella term that groups together a variety of people whose gender identity differs from their birth sex (Pew Research Center, *A Survey of LGBT Americans—Attitudes, Experiences and Values in Changing Times*, Washington, D.C., June 13, 2013, p. 15). Issues faced by transgender individuals in the workplace are frequently included in research regarding lesbian, gay, and bisexual (LGB) individuals. Although some data that we present include the perceptions of transgender employees and our recommendations may also pertain to those individuals, the focus of this report is on sexual orientation. Issues relating to transgender employees in the workplace are sufficiently different from those facing LGB employees as to require separate, focused research.

[2] In this historical discussion, we use the term "homosexual" as it was the norm at the time and used by our many sources. In other Sections, we use the terms "LGBT," "lesbian," "gay," and "bisexual," as today "homosexual" is seen by some as an outdated term that,

historically, was used to "pathologize" gay and lesbian individuals (University of California, Davis LGBT Resource Center Glossary at www.lgbtcenter.ucdavis.edu/lgbt-education/lgbtqia-glossary).

[3] Gregory B. Lewis, "Lifting the Ban on Gays in the Civil Service: Federal Policy Toward Gay and Lesbian Employees since the Cold War," *Public Administration Review*, September/October 1997, p. 387. This organization was the Society for Human Rights founded by Henry Gerber and chartered by the State of Illinois on December 10, 1924 (Jonathan Katz, *Gay American History—Lesbians and Gay Men in the U.S.A.*, Thomas Y. Crowell Company, New York, 1976, pp. 385-393; and St. Sukie de la Croix, *Chicago Whispers: A History of LGBT Chicago Before Stonewall*, The University of Wisconsin Press, Madison, 2012, pp. 82-84).

[4] Lewis, op. cit., p. 387.

[5] See, for example, David K. Johnson, *The Lavender Scare: The Cold War Persecution of Gays and Lesbians in the Federal Government*, The University of Chicago Press, Chicago, 2006, p. 6.

[6] American Psychiatric Association, *Diagnostic and Statistical Manual of Mental Disorders*, 1952, pp. 38-39. In 1975, the American Psychological Association adopted a resolution supporting this change (Jj. Conger, "Proceedings of the American Psychological Association, Incorporated for the Year 1974: Minutes of the Annual Meeting of the Council of Representatives," *American Psychologist*, June 1975, pp. 620-651). Today, all major professional mental health organizations have affirmed that homosexuality is not a mental disorder (American Psychiatric Association website, www.psychiatry.org/lgbt-sexual-orientation).

[7] "Perverts Called Government Peril," *The New York Times*, April 19, 1950, p. 25.

[8] Johnson, op. cit., p. 2.

[9] Id., p. 6. The Congressman was Representative George Christopher of Missouri.

[10] Tim Weiner, *Enemies: A History of the FBI*, Random House Trade Paperback, 2013, p. 175.

[11] Id., pp. 174-175. See also, Julian E. Barnes, "The Third Man," *U.S. News and World Report*, January 27-February 3, 2003, pp. 61-62; and Andrew Pierce and Stephen Adams, "Anthony Blunt: Confessions of Spy Who Passed Secrets to Russia During the War," *The Telegraph*, July 22, 2009. The members of the ring were Donald Maclean, Guy Burgess, John Cairncross, Kim Philby, and Anthony Blunt. Although two members of the group defected in 1951, suspicion was cast on the remaining members until the last of the group confessed to his involvement in 1964.

[12] Randolph W. Baxter, "'Homo-Hunting' in the Early Cold War: Senator Kenneth Wherry and the Homophobic Side of McCarthyism," *Nebraska History*, Fall 2003, p. 119.

[13] S. Rep. No. 81-241 (1950).

[14] Lewis, op. cit., p. 388. See also Johnson, op. cit., p. 17. Twenty-two of these 91 employees found employment in other agencies. Following these hearings, the U.S. Civil Service Commission initiated investigations on these 22 employees and obtained resignations in all but 1 case (Johnson, op. cit., p. 81).

[15] S. Rep. No. 81-241, op. cit., p. 1.

[16] Id., p. 8.

[17] Id., p. 9.

[18] Id., pp. 7-8.

[19] Id., p. 8.

[20] Id., p. 3.

[21] Lewis, op. cit., p. 388.

[22] S. Rep. No. 81-241, op. cit., p. 4.
[23] Id.
[24] Id.
[25] Id.
[26] Katz, op. cit., p. 96. The Senator was Kenneth Wherry of Nebraska who led the Senate appropriations subcommittee investigative effort referenced earlier in this Section.
[27] S. Rep. No. 81-241, op. cit., p. 10.
[28] Id., pp. 10-11.
[29] "Government Employment and the Homosexual (*Norton v. Macy, Morrison v. State Board of Education*)," *St. John's Law Review*, December 1970, p. 303. In 1961, Illinois became the first State to abandon its sodomy law when it adopted a comprehensive revision to its criminal code. That revision followed the 1955 recommendations of the American Law Institute, a group of distinguished law professors and lawyers (*Lawrence v. Texas*, 539 U.S. 558 (2003)).
[30] S. Rep. No. 81-241, op. cit., p. 13.
[31] "Government-Created Employment Disabilities of the Homosexual," *Harvard Law Review*, June 1969, p. 1742.
[32] Id.
[33] Id.
[34] S. Rep. No. 81-241, op. cit., p. 19.
[35] Johnson, op. cit., pp. 83-84; quoting Senators Homer Ferguson of Michigan and Styles Bridges of New Hampshire and Congressmen John J. Rooney of New York and Arthur Miller of Nebraska.
[36] Id., p. 84.
[37] Weiner, op. cit., p. 149.
[38] Landon R. Y. Storrs, *The Second Red Scare and the Unmaking of the New Deal Left*, Princeton University Press, Princeton, 2013, p. 111. Executive Order 10241 was titled, *Amending Executive Order No. 9835 Entitled, "Prescribing Procedures for the Administration of an Employees Loyalty Program in the Executive Branch of the Government."*
[39] Compare Executive Order 9835 Part V ("The standard for the refusal of employment or the removal from employment in an executive department or agency on grounds relating to loyalty shall be that, on all the evidence, reasonable grounds exist for *belief that the person involved is disloyal* to the Government of the United States.") with Executive Order 10241 ("The standard for the refusal of employment or the removal from employment in an executive department or agency on grounds relating to loyalty shall be that, on all the evidence, there is a *reasonable doubt as to the loyalty of the person* involved to the Government of the United States."). (Italics added.)
[40] Storrs, op. cit., p. 111.
[41] Lewis, op. cit., p. 389.
[42] The actual period of time covered was May 28, 1953, through June 30, 1954. U.S. Civil Service Commission, *1954 Annual Report*, Washington, D.C., 1954, p. 135.
[43] Terminations or resignations for sex perversion totaled 840 for the time period May 28, 1953, through June 30, 1955. "Risk Dismissals are Put at 3,614," *The New York Times*, September 27, 1955, p. 30.
[44] Weiner, op. cit., pp. 175-176.
[45] Id., pp. 213-214.
[46] Id., pp. 214-215.

[47] Johnson, op. cit., pp. 196. This question was asked on the Report of Medical History (Standard Form 89) portion of the application for employment.

[48] Letter from John W. Macy, Jr., Chairman, U.S. Civil Service Commission, to The Mattachine Society of Washington, (Feb. 25, 1966), p. 1. As cited in *Perry v. Schwarzenegger*, 704 F.Supp. 2d 921, 1004 (N.D. Cal. 2010) and accessed at www.kamenypapers.org.

[49] Id., p. 2.

[50] Id., p. 3.

[51] Id.

[52] Id.

[53] Id.

[54] Johnson, op. cit., p. 204.

[55] *Harvard Law Review*, op. cit., pp. 1741-1742.

[56] Lewis, op. cit., p. 391.

[57] Id.

[58] 317 F.2d 582 (D.C. Cir. 1963).

[59] Id. at 583.

[60] Id. at 587.

[61] Id.

[62] 349 F.2d 182 (D.C. Cir. 1965).

[63] Id. at 183.

[64] Id. at 182-183.

[65] Id. at 184-185.

[66] Id. at 185.

[67] *Scott v. Macy*, 402 F.2d 644, 647 (D.C. Cir. 1968).

[68] Id. at 645.

[69] Id. at 649.

[70] Id. U.S. Civil Service Commission Federal Personnel Manual System, Section 2-4(a) (2), Inst. 85, Jan. 27, 1967; as referenced in the decision.

[71] 417 F.2d 1161 (D.C. Cir. 1969).

[72] Id. at 1162.

[73] Id. at 1165.

[74] Id. at 1166.

[75] Lewis, op. cit., p. 392.

[76] Johnson, op. cit., p. 209.

[77] 63 F.R.D. 399 (N.D. Cal. 1973), *aff'd on other grounds*, 528 F.2d 905 (9th Cir. 1975).

[78] Id. at 400.

[79] Id. at 401. For an example of the separation of an employee based on off-duty misconduct that adversely affected the efficiency of the service being upheld, see *Brown v. Department of the Navy*, 229 F.3d 1356 (Fed. Cir. 2000).

[80] Baxter, op. cit., p. 128.

[81] Lewis, op. cit., p. 389.

[82] *Society*, 63 F.R.D. at 402.

[83] "Fairness for Homosexuals," *The Washington Post*, February 2, 1971, p. A14.

[84] U.S. Civil Service Commission, *Challenge and Change: 85th Annual Report*, Washington, D.C., 1968, p. 38.

[85] U.S. Civil Service Commission, *A Pace Setting Year for Personnel Management: 88th Annual Report*, Washington, D.C., 1971, pp. 48-49.

[86] "Homosexual Hiring is Revised by U.S.," *The New York Times*, July 4, 1975, p. 45.

[87] "Shedding Blinders," *The New York Times*, July 16, 1975, p. 36.

[88] Pub. L. No. 95-454, 92 Stat. 1111.

[89] Office of Special Counsel, U.S. Merit Systems Protection Board, *Protecting the Integrity of the Merit System: A Legislative History of the Merit System Principles, Prohibited Personnel Practices and the Office of the Special Counsel*, 1985, p. vii.

[90] Two additional PPPs have since been defined, one by the Veterans Employment Opportunity Act of 1998 (Pub. L. No. 105-339, 112 Stat. 3182) and one by the Whistleblower Protection Enhancement Act of 2012 (Pub. L. No. 112-199, 126 Stat. 1465).

[91] 5 U.S.C. § 2302(b)(10).

[92] S. Rep. No. 95-1272, p. 131 (1978) (Conf. Rep.).

[93] H.R. 11280 95th Cong. (1978), § 2302(b)(10).

[94] See for example: Margot Canady, "'Who is a Homosexual?' The Consolidation of Sexual Identities in MidTwentieth-Century American Immigration Law," *Law and Social Inquiry*, Spring 2003, p. 359.

[95] S. Rep. No. 95-1272, op. cit., p. 131.

[96] Office of the Special Counsel, op. cit., p. 121.

[97] Lewis, op. cit., p. 393.

[98] S. Rep. No. 81-241, op. cit., p. 10.

[99] Theodore B. Olson, "Termination of an Assistant United States Attorney on Grounds Related to His Acknowledged Homosexuality," *Opinions of the Office of Legal Counsel of the United States Department of Justice*, Volume 7, 1983, p. 46.

[100] Id., p. 47.

[101] Id., p. 46.

[102] Lewis, op. cit., p. 393.

[103] Rosalie A. Cameron Memorandum for Directors of Personnel, "Policy Statement on Discrimination on the Basis of Conduct Which Does Not Adversely Affect the Performance of Employees or Applicants for Employment," March 10, 1997.

[104] 5 U.S.C. § 1214(b) and (h). See also OSC Form 53 (March 2008). For an example of such a complaint, see OSC Press Release PR03 13, "U.S. Office of Special Counsel Secures Corrective and Disciplinary Action in Case of Federal Job Applicant Denied Job Because of His Homosexuality," June 20, 2003. Accessed at www.osc.gov.

[105] Nondiscrimination Provisions (Proposed rule), 78 Fed. Reg. 54,434 (September 4, 2013).

[106] 5 U.S.C. § 2302(b)(12).

[107] S. Rep. 95-969, pp. 22-23 (1978 U.S.C.C.A.N. 2723, 2745).

[108] *Special Counsel v. Lynn*, 29 M.S.P.R. 666, 668-670 (1986). At the time of this case, what is now 5 U.S.C. § 2302(b)(12) was numbered (b)(11).

[109] See *Lawrence*, 539 U.S. at 567 (holding that "[w]hen sexuality finds overt expression in intimate conduct with another person, the conduct can be but one element in a personal bond that is more enduring. The liberty protected by the Constitution allows homosexual persons the right to make this choice."). MSPB has not yet received a case in which the constitutional right to such private conduct has been raised with respect to 5 U.S.C. § 2302(b)(12).

[110] An earlier executive order signed by President Clinton barred denying security clearances to Federal employees or contractors based solely on their sexual orientation. See Executive Order 12968, *Access to Classified Information,* August 2, 1995.

[111] Statement on Signing an Executive Order on Equal Employment Opportunity in the Federal Government, 34 Weekly Comp. Pres. Docs. 994 (May 28, 1998).

[112] As provided for by Executive Order 11478, August 8, 1969.

[113] Equal Employment Opportunity Commission Fact Sheet FSE/16, *Discrimination Based on Sexual Orientation, Status as a Parent, Marital Status and Political Affiliation*, accessed at www.eeoc.gov/eeoc/publications/index.cfm.

[114] Statement on Signing an Executive Order on Equal Employment Opportunity in the Federal Government, op. cit.

[115] Executive Order 13152, *Further Amendment to Executive Order 11478, Equal Employment Opportunity in Federal Government*, May 2, 2000.

[116] Equal Employment Opportunity Commission Fact Sheet FSE/16, op. cit.

[117] Accessed at www.chcoc.gov/transmittals.

[118] Statement on Signing a Memorandum on Federal Benefits and Non-Discrimination and Support of Domestic Partners Benefits and Obligations Legislation, Daily Comp. Pres. Docs., 2009 DCPD No. 00476, p. 1 (June 17, 2009). The ambassador was Michael Guest.

[119] Id.

[120] Memorandum of June 17, 2009, Federal Benefits and Non-Discrimination, 74 Fed. Reg. 29,393 (June 22, 2009).

[121] Statement on Signing a Memorandum on Federal Benefits and Non-Discrimination and Support of Domestic Partners Benefits and Obligations Legislation, op. cit., p. 2.

[122] Memorandum of June 2, 2010, Extension of Benefits to Same-Sex Domestic Partners of Federal Employees, 75 Fed. Reg. 32,247 (June 8, 2010).

[123] Agency Use of Appropriated Funds for Child Care Costs for Lower Income Employees (Final rule), 77 Fed. Reg. 42,905 (July 20, 2012).

[124] Id.

[125] Noncompetitive Appointment of Certain Former Overseas Employees (Final rule), 77 Fed. Reg. 42,902 (July 20, 2012).

[126] Presumption of Insurable Interest for Same-Sex Domestic Partners (Final rule), 77 Fed. Reg. 42,909 (July 20, 2012).

[127] Change in Definitions; Evacuation Pay and the Separate Maintenance Allowance at Johnston Island (Final rule), 77 Fed. Reg. 42,903 (July 20, 2012).

[128] John Berry Memorandum for Chief Human Capital Officers, "Extension of 24-Hour LWOP Family Support Policy to Same-Sex Domestic Partners of Federal Employees," September 10, 2010. Accessed at www.chcoc.gov/ transmittals.

[129] Absence and Leave; Definitions of Family Member, Immediate Relative, and Related Terms (Final rule), 75 Fed. Reg. 33,491 (June 14, 2010).

[130] Federal Travel Regulation (FTR); Terms and Definitions for "Dependent", "Domestic Partner", "Domestic Partnership", and "Immediate Family" (Final rule), 76 Fed. Reg. 59,914 (September 28, 2011).

[131] Federal Long Term Care Insurance Program: Eligibility Changes (Final rule), 75 Fed. Reg. 30,267 (June 1, 2010).

[132] For further information on the extension of benefits, see John Berry Report for the President, "Extending Federal Employment Benefits to Same-Sex Domestic Partners of Federal Employees," April 1, 2011.

[133] Pub. L. No. 104-199, 110 Stat. 2419 and 2420.

[134] *United States v. Windsor*, 133 S. Ct. 2675, 2696 (2013).

[135] Elaine Kaplan Memorandum for Heads of Executive Departments and Agencies, "Guidance on the Extension of Benefits to Married Gay and Lesbian Federal Employees, Annuitants, and Their Families," June 28, 2013. Accessed at www.chcoc.gov/transmittals. See also, Federal Employees Health Benefits Program and Federal Employees Dental and Vision Insurance Program: Expanding Coverage of Children; Federal Flexible Benefits Plan: Pre-

Tax Payment of Health Benefits Premiums: Conforming Amendments (Final rule), 78 Fed. Reg. 64,873 (October 30, 2013). For an example of litigation involving these benefits changes, see, *Hara v. Office of Personnel Management*, No. 2009-3141 (Fed. Cir. Sep. 16, 2013) vacating MSPB's decision that the Defense of Marriage Act barred grant of a survivor annuity and remanding the case to MSPB for proceedings consistent with *Windsor*.

[136] U.S. Office of Personnel Management, *Guidance for Agency-Specific Diversity and Inclusion Strategic Plans*, November 2011, p. 4.

[137] Id., p. 3.

[138] Human Rights Campaign Foundation, *Corporate Equality Index 2013*, Washington, D.C., 2012, p. 8.

[139] U.S. Government Accountability Office, *Sexual Orientation and Gender Identity Employment Discrimination: Overview of State Statutes and Complaint Data*, GAO-10-135R, October 1, 2009.

[140] Pew Research Center, op. cit., p. 108. Based on a nationally representative 2013 online research panel of 398 gay men, 277 lesbians, 479 bisexuals, and 43 transgender individuals.

[141] Lydia Saad, "Americans Evenly Divided on Morality of Homosexuality," Gallup, Inc., June 2008. Accessed at www.gallup.com/poll/108115/Americans-Evenly-Divided-Morality-Homosexuality.aspx. Based on telephone interviews with 1,017 adults across the country in 2008.

[142] Brief of 278 businesses; law and professional firms; trade and civic organizations; and cities, counties and the United States Conference of Mayors as *amici curiae* for respondent in *Windsor* at 35.

[143] Diane Cadrain, "Sexual Equity in the Workplace," *HR Magazine*, September 2008, pp. 44-50.

[144] Ronald J. Alsop, "Pride vs. Prejudice," *Workforce Management*, March 2011, p. 42.

[145] Cadrain, op. cit. Although many studies support the link between LGBT-supportive policies and workforce outcomes, none provide direct quantitative estimates of that link to the bottom line (M.V. Lee Badgett, Laura E. Durso, Angeliki Kastanis, and Christy Mallory, "The Business Impact of LGBT-Supportive Workplace Policies," The Williams Institute, UCLA School of Law, May 2013).

[146] Survey data regarding employee perceptions of discrimination cannot be equated with actual incidents of discrimination. Survey responses reflect the respondent's interpretation of events. Respondents may have differing ideas about what constitutes discrimination that not only differ from each other but also differ from any legal definition of discrimination. Nevertheless, the survey data presented in this Section represent Federal employee perceptions and attitudes that may affect virtually every aspect of an employee's daily work life from effectively accomplishing tasks to contributing to a positive work environment.

[147] The MPS 2010 was distributed to 71,970 full-time, permanent Federal employees in 24 agencies. We received valid responses from 42,020 individuals, for a response rate of 58 percent. For more information about this survey, see: U.S. Merit Systems Protection Board, *Federal Employee Engagement: The Motivating Potential of Job Characteristics and Rewards*, December 2012.

[148] U.S. Merit Systems Protection Board, *Prohibited Personnel Practices: Employee Perceptions*, Washington, D.C., August 2011, pp. 35-36.

[149] Id., p. 36.

[150] The MPS 2005 was distributed to about 74,000 full-time, permanent Federal employees in 24 agencies. We received valid responses from 36,926 individuals for a response rate of approximately 50 percent. For more information about the MPS 2005, see: U.S. Merit Systems Protection Board, *Accomplishing Our Mission: Results of the Merit Principles*

Survey 2005, February 2007. The MPS 2007 was distributed to 68,789 full-time, permanent, Federal employees in 30 agencies. We received valid responses from 41,577 individuals, for a response rate of 60 percent. For more information about the MPS 2007, see: U.S. Merit Systems Protection Board, *Managing for Engagement – Communication, Connection, and Courage*, July 2009. See note 147 for information about the MPS 2010.

[151] The wording of these survey questions has changed over the years: The MPS 2005 asked: "In the past 2 years, do you feel you have been denied a job, promotion, pay or other job benefit because of unlawful discrimination based upon sexual orientation?" The MPS 2007 asked: "In the past 2 years, have you been denied a job, promotion, pay increase, or other job benefit because of unlawful discrimination based on sexual orientation?" The MPS 2010 asked: "In the past two years, an agency official (e.g. supervisor, manager, senior leader, etc.) in my work unit has discriminated in favor or against someone in a personnel action based upon sexual orientation." The one percent figure refers to affirmative responses to these questions. See, for example, U.S. Merit Systems Protection Board, *Prohibited Personnel Practices: Employee Perceptions*, Washington, D.C., August 2011, p. 34.

[152] U.S. Merit Systems Protection Board, *Prohibited Personnel Practices: Employee Perceptions*, Washington, D.C., August 2011, pp. 35-36.

[153] FEVS question 38, *2012 Federal Employee Viewpoint Survey Results—Report by Demographics*, U.S. Office of Personnel Management, p. 112.

[154] Gregory M. Herek, "Hate Crimes and Stigma-Related Experiences Among Sexual Minority Adults in the United States: Prevalence Estimates from a National Probability Sample," *Journal of Interpersonal Violence*, January 2009, pp. 54-74. Based on a 2005 survey of 662 lesbian, gay, and bisexual individuals.

[155] Pew Research Center, op. cit., p. 42.

[156] U.S. Merit Systems Protection Board, *The Power of Federal Employee Engagement*, Washington, D.C., September 2008.

[157] U.S. Merit Systems Protection Board, *Prohibited Personnel Practices: Employee Perceptions*, Washington, D.C., August 2011, pp. 37-38.

[158] 5 U.S.C. § 1215(a)(3)(A).

[159] Pub. L. No. 107-174. Also known as the "No FEAR Act."

[160] For further information, see U.S. Equal Employment Opportunity Commission, *Questions and Answers: No FEAR Act*, accessed at www.eeoc.gov/eeoc/statistics/nofear/qanda.cfm.

[161] Implementation of Title II of the Notification and Federal Employee Antidiscrimination and Retaliation Act of 2002—Notification and Training (Final rule), 71 Fed. Reg. 41,098 (Jul. 20, 2006). See regulations at 5 C.F.R. § 724.202.

[162] Id., p. 41,095.

[163] The MPS 2010 asked respondents whether their agency had educated them about what their rights would be if they disclosed wrongdoing—another activity required by the No FEAR Act. Only 55 percent of respondents agreed they had received such education, see U.S. Merit Systems Protection Board, *Blowing the Whistle: Barriers to Federal Employees Making Disclosures,* Washington, D.C., November, 2011, p. 14.

[164] Data received from OPM for analysis were collapsed into the following three categories: heterosexual or straight, LGBT, I prefer not to say. Although issues related to gender identity fall outside the scope of this report, 2012 FEVS data made available by OPM for review included perceptions of transgender employees.

[165] U.S. Office of Personnel Management, *2012 Federal Employee Viewpoint Survey Results—Governmentwide Management Report,* p. 2. For more information about the FEVS, including obtaining survey data, see www. fedview.opm.gov.

[166] Employees of the very smallest agencies were not asked demographic questions including their sexual orientation to protect their privacy (U.S. Office of Personnel Management, *2012 Federal Employee Viewpoint Survey Results—Technical Report*, p. 40; and 2012 FEVS Small Agency Management Reports noting that agencies that had 50 or more survey-eligible employees had the option to include the demographic section on the 2012 FEVS).

[167] For an explanation of OPM's 2012 FEVS weighting strategy, see *2012 Federal Employee Viewpoint Survey Results—Technical Report*, op. cit., pp. 24-25.

[168] OPM adheres to a strict practice of not releasing data that would compromise the privacy of any survey respondent group so the number of demographic variables made available for analysis was limited.

[169] *2012 Federal Employee Viewpoint Survey Results—Governmentwide Management Report*, op. cit., p. 28.

[170] Gary J. Gates, "How many people are lesbian, gay, bisexual, and transgender?," The Williams Institute, UCLA School of Law, April 2011, estimating 3.5 percent of adults identify as lesbian, gay, or bisexual, and 0.3 percent identify as transgender. See also, Gary J. Gates and Frank Newport, "LGBT Percentage Highest in D.C., Lowest in North Dakota," Gallup.com, February 15, 2013, estimating the nationwide average of adults who identify as LGBT at 3.5 percent.

[171] Unweighted 2012 FEVS results.

[172] U.S. Office of Personnel Management, *2012 Federal Employee Viewpoint Survey Results—Report on Demographic Questions by Agency*, pp. 16-20.

[173] Human Rights Campaign Foundation, *Degrees of Equality—A National Study Examining Workplace Climate for LGBT Employees*, Washington, D.C., 2009, pp. 15, 33. Based on a 2008 survey of 761 LGBT individuals.

[174] For more information on HCAAF, see www.opm.gov/policy-data-oversight/human-capital-management/.

[175] *2012 Federal Employee Viewpoint Survey Results—Governmentwide Management Report*, op. cit., pp. 5-13.

[176] Id., p. 34.

[177] Id., p. 22.

[178] For lists of questions comprising each index, see *2012 Federal Employee Viewpoint Survey Results— Governmentwide Management Report,* op. cit., pp. 41-57. For LGBT and non-LGBT responses to those questions, see *2012 Federal Employee Viewpoint Survey Results—Report by Demographics*, op. cit., pp. 1-211.

[179] These three groupings and their component 2012 FEVS questions merely illustrate that differences exist in the attitudes of LGBT employees across different agencies—differences may exist in other areas as well.

[180] See the Appendix for further information about how we determined the effect of the 2012 FEVS LGBT item on other survey items, why we selected these 16 questions to discuss, and why we placed questions in selected groups.

[181] Data represent four agencies with at least 100 FEVS respondents who self-identified as LGBT.

[182] Data represent three agencies with at least 100 FEVS respondents who self-identified as LGBT.

[183] Data represent one agency with at least 100 FEVS respondents who self-identified as LGBT.

[184] Human Rights Campaign Foundation, 2009, op. cit., p. 11.

[185] Id., p. 5.

[186] U.S. Merit Systems Protection Board, "Religion in the Workplace: Moving Beyond Nondiscrimination and Accommodation," *Issues of Merit*, July 2011, p. 5.

[187] H.R. 3128, 109th Cong. (2005). This legislation was not passed by either house of Congress.

[188] EEOC has jurisdiction over employment discrimination codified in a number of laws prohibiting discrimination based on race, color, sex, religion, national origin, age, disability, and genetic information. See 29 C.F.R. § 1614.101 (a) and (b).

[189] *Mahaffey v. Department of Agriculture*, 105 M.S.P.R. 347, ¶ 24 (2007) and Matthew S. Bajko, "Federal Agency Quietly Reasserts Pro-Gay Policy," *The Bay Area Reporter*, September 24, 2009.

[190] Christopher Lee, "Official Says Law Doesn't Cover Gays," *The Washington Post,* May 25, 2005, p. A25; and Stephen Barr, "Bills Would Affirm Anti-Bias Laws Cover Sexual Orientation," *The Washington Post*, May 15, 2007, p. D4.

[191] Wayne Washington, "White House, Counsel Split on Gay Rights—Official Had Questioned Antidiscrimination Law," *Boston Globe*, April 1, 2004. p. A4.

[192] H.R. Rep. No. 109-313 (2005).

[193] "Domestic Partner Benefits: Fair Policy and Good Business for the Federal Government," Hearing before the Committee on Homeland Security and Governmental Affairs United States Senate, S. Hrg. 111-758, October 15, 2009, p. 29.

[194] Some employees may have other protections or avenues of redress within their agencies by virtue of negotiated collective bargaining agreements.

[195] Congressional Research Service, *Sexual Orientation and Gender Identity Discrimination in Employment: A Legal Analysis of the Employment Non-Discrimination Act (ENDA)*, July 15, 2013, p. 4. See *Oncale v. Sundowner Offshore Services*, 523 U.S. 75 (1998) and *Price Waterhouse v. Hopkins*, 490 U.S. 228 (1989).

[196] U.S. Equal Employment Opportunity Commission, *Processing Complaints of Discrimination by Lesbian, Gay, Bisexual, and Transgender (LGBT) Federal Employees*. Accessed at www.eeoc.gov//federal/directives/lgbt_ complaint_processing.cfm.

[197] See, e.g., *Brooker v. U.S. Postal Service*, EEOC Appeal No. 0120112085 (2013).

[198] See, e.g., *Veretto v. U.S. Postal Service*, EEOC Appeal No. 0120110873 (2011).

[199] See, for example, (a) "Nominations of Othoniel Armendariz to be a Member of the Federal Labor Relations Authority and Kay Coles James to be Director of the Office of Personnel Management," Hearing before the Committee on Governmental Affairs United States Senate, S. Hrg. 107-128, June 21, 2001, p. 89. (b) "Nominations of Hon. Linda M. Springer, to be Director, U.S. Office of Personnel Management; Hon. Laura A. Cordero, to be Associate Judge, Superior Court of the District of Columbia; and Hon. Noel Anketell Kramer, to be Associate Judge, District of Columbia Court of Appeals," Hearing before the Committee on Homeland Security and Governmental Affairs United States Senate, S. Hrg. 109-156, June 15, 2005, p. 61. (c) "Nomination of Carolyn N. Lerner to be Special Counsel, Office of Special Counsel," Hearing before the Committee on Homeland Security and Governmental Affairs United States Senate, S. Hrg. 112-218, March 10, 2011, p. 37.

[200] U.S. Office of Personnel Management, *Guidance for Agency-Specific Diversity and Inclusion Strategic Plans*, November 2011, p. 16.

[201] Human Rights Campaign Foundation, 2012, op. cit., p. 33.

[202] U.S. Merit Systems Protection Board, *The Federal Government: A Model Employer or a Work in Progress? Perspectives from 25 Years of the Merit Principles Survey*, September 2008, p. 55.

[203] Human Rights Campaign Foundation, 2009, op. cit., p. 37.

[204] U.S. Merit Systems Protection Board, *Women in the Federal Government: Ambitions and Achievements*, Washington, D.C., May 2011, p. 60.

[205] Id.

[206] 5 U.S.C. § 2301(b)(2) and (8).

[207] 5 U.S.C. § 2301(b)(1).

[208] Executive Order 13583, *Establishing a Coordinated Government-Wide Initiative to Promote Diversity and Inclusion in the Federal Workforce*, August 18, 2011.

[209] Robert F. DeVellis, *Scale Development Theory and Applications* (2nd ed.), Sage Publications, Thousand Oaks, CA, 2003, pp. 103-104.

In: Federal Employees and Sexual Orientation ISBN: 978-1-63484-376-8
Editor: Ross Henderson

Chapter 2

UPDATE ON STATE STATUTES AND ADMINISTRATIVE COMPLAINT DATA ON EMPLOYMENT DISCRIMINATION BASED ON SEXUAL ORIENTATION AND GENDER IDENTITY*

U.S. Government Accountability Office

The Honorable Tom Harkin
Chairman
Committee on Health, Education,
Labor, and Pensions United States Senate

The Honorable Mark Kirk
United States Senate

The Honorable Jeffrey A. Merkley
United States Senate

Federal law prohibits discrimination in employment based on a number of factors, including race, color, religion, sex, national origin, disability, and age. We reported most recently in 2009 that although federal law does not prohibit

---

* This is an edited, reformatted and augmented version of a U.S. Government Accountability Office publication, No. GAO-13-700R, dated July 31, 2013.

employment discrimination on the basis of sexual orientation, some states provide such protection by statute.[1] Specifically, we reported that 22 states had statutes explicitly prohibiting employment discrimination on the basis of sexual orientation; we also reported that 13 states had statutes explicitly prohibiting employment discrimination on the basis of gender identity.[2] In addition, we reported that, generally, the administrative complaint data reported by states at that time showed relatively few employment discrimination complaints based on sexual orientation and gender identity.

In response to your request, this letter updates our 2009 report with regard to the number of states with statutes explicitly prohibiting employment discrimination based on sexual orientation and gender identity.[3] We also include data provided by those states on the number of administrative complaints related to employment discrimination filed between 2007 and 2012— specifically, the total number of complaints and the number of complaints listing sexual orientation or gender identity as a claimed basis for discrimination. We found that no states have added explicit statutory prohibitions against employment discrimination based on sexual orientation since our 2009 report was issued, leaving the total number of states with such protections at 22.[4] In addition, we found that five states— Connecticut, Delaware, Hawaii, Massachusetts, and Nevada—have added explicit employment discrimination prohibitions on the basis of gender identity since our 2009 report was issued, bringing the total number of states with such protections to 18.[5] There is significant overlap in the states protecting individuals from employment discrimination on the bases of sexual orientation and gender identity. Eighteen states have statutes that explicitly prohibit both sexual orientation- and gender identity-based employment discrimination, while four states have such prohibitions only for employment discrimination based on sexual orientation. With respect to complaint data, consistent with what we reported in 2009, the administrative complaint data reported to us by states for 2007 through 2012 show relatively few employment discrimination complaints based on sexual orientation and gender identity.

To complete this work, we utilized legal databases to determine which states have statutes explicitly prohibiting employment discrimination on the basis of sexual orientation or gender identity.[6] We sent questionnaires to cognizant officials in the 22 states we identified as having such laws and asked them to verify that we had identified the relevant statutory provisions.[7] We also asked them to provide the total number of administrative employment discrimination complaints filed for the most recent 7 years[8] for which data were available, as well as the number of complaints that identified sexual orientation or gender identity as one of the claimed bases for employment discrimination.[9] All complaint data presented in the enclosure that follows are as reported to us by state officials; we did not independently verify the accuracy of these data or review the methodologies used by states to compile data. We created a table for each state incorporating their responses to our questionnaire and sent the tables to state officials for their comments, which we incorporated as appropriate.

Enclosed with this correspondence are tables for each of the 22 states for which we compiled information. These tables convey, for each state, the responses to our questionnaire— specifically, a citation to the relevant state statutory provisions, as well as the reported employment discrimination complaint data. James M. Rebbe and Lincoln Schroth, Senior Attorneys, and Sheila R. McCoy, Assistant General Counsel, prepared this letter.

Sincerely yours, Helen T. Desaulniers
Managing Associate General Counsel

ENCLOSURE

CALIFORNIA	
Statutory provision(s) providing protection from employment discrimination on the basis of sexual orientation	Cal. Gov. Code § 12940
Statutory provision(s) providing protection from employment discrimination on the basis of gender identity	Cal. Gov. Code § 12940[10]
Total number of employment discrimination administrative complaints filed between 2007 and 2012[11]	CY 2012: 19,839 CY 2011: 18,012 CY 2010: 18,335 CY 2009: 17,680 CY 2008: 18,786 CY 2007: 16,396
Total number of employment discrimination administrative complaints filed between 2007 and 2012 where at least one of the claimed bases for discrimination is sexual orientation	CY 2012: 1,104 CY 2011: 727 CY 2010: 717 CY 2009: 807 CY 2008: 821 CY 2007: 815
Total number of employment discrimination administrative complaints filed between 2007 and 2012 where at least one of the claimed bases for discrimination is gender identity	Not available[12]

COLORADO	
Statutory provision(s) providing protection from employment discrimination on the basis of sexual orientation	Colo. Rev. Stat. § 24-34-402
Statutory provision(s) providing protection from employment discrimination on the basis of gender identity	Colo. Rev. Stat. §§ 24-34-401(7.5) and 24-34-402[13]
Total number of employment discrimination administrative complaints filed between 2007 and 2012[14]	FY 2011-2012: 516 FY 2010-2011: 575 FY 2009-2010: 599 FY 2008-2009: 712 FY 2007-2008: 635 FY 2006-2007: 593
Total number of employment discrimination administrative complaints filed between 2007 and 2012 where at least one of the claimed bases for discrimination is sexual orientation[15]	FY 2011-2012: 35 FY 2010-2011: 41 FY 2009-2010: 33 FY 2008-2009: 34 FY 2007-2008: 21
Total number of employment discrimination administrative complaints filed between 2007 and 2012 where at least one of the claimed bases for discrimination is gender identity	FY 2011-2012: 1 FY 2010-2011: 1 FY 2009-2010: 2 FY 2008-2009: 3 FY 2007-2008: 2

CONNECTICUT	
Statutory provision(s) providing protection from employment discrimination on the basis of sexual orientation	Conn. Gen. Stat. § 46a-81c
Statutory provision(s) providing protection from employment discrimination on the basis of gender identity	Conn. Gen. Stat. § 46a-60[16]
Total number of employment discrimination administrative complaints filed between 2007 and 2012[17]	CY 2012: 1,653 CY 2011: 1,656 CY 2010: 1,390 FY 2009-2010: 1,836 FY 2008-2009: 1,827 FY 2007-2008: 1,946 FY 2006-2007: 1,878
Total number of employment discrimination administrative complaints filed between 2007 and 2012 where at least one of the claimed bases for discrimination is sexual orientation	CY 2012: 41 CY 2011: 49 CY 2010: 36 FY 2009-2010: 53 FY 2008-2009: 44 FY 2007-2008: 49 FY 2006-2007: 60
Total number of employment discrimination administrative complaints filed between 2007 and 2012 where at least one of the claimed bases for discrimination is gender identity	Not available[18]

DELAWARE	
Statutory provision(s) providing protection from employment discrimination on the basis of sexual orientation	19 Del. C. § 711
Statutory provision(s) providing protection from employment discrimination on the basis of gender identity	19 Del. C. § 711[19]
Total number of employment discrimination-administrative complaints filed between 2007 and 2012[20]	FY 2012: 727 FY 2011: 520 FY 2010: 437 FY 2009: 654 FY 2008: 665 FY 2007: 653
Total number of employment discrimination administrative complaints filed between 2007 and 2012 where at least one of the claimed bases for discrimination is sexual orientation[21]	FY 2012: 31 FY 2011: 16 FY 2010: 13
Total number of employment discrimination administrative complaints filed between 2007 and 2012 where at least one of the claimed bases for discrimination is gender identity	Not available[22]

DISTRICT OF COLUMBIA	
Statutory provision(s) providing protection from employment discrimination on the basis of sexual orientation	D.C. Code § 2-1402.11
Statutory provision(s) providing protection from employment discrimination on the basis of gender identity	D.C. Code § 2-1402.11[23]
Total number of employment discrimination administrative complaints filed between 2007 and 2012[24]	FY 2012: 279 FY 2011: 339 FY 2010: 415 FY 2009: 488 FY 2008: 357 FY 2007: 282
Total number of employment discrimination administrative complaints filed between 2007 and 2012 where at least one of the claimed bases for discrimination is sexual orientation	FY 2012: 15 FY 2011: 18 FY 2010: 21 FY 2009: 24 FY 2008: 28 FY 2007: 17
Total number of employment discrimination administrative complaints filed between 2007 and 2012 where at least one of the claimed bases for discrimination is gender identity	FY 2012: 0 FY 2011: 0 FY 2010: 1 FY 2009: 1 FY 2008: 2 FY 2007: 0

HAWAII	
Statutory provision(s) providing protection from employment discrimination on the basis of sexual orientation	H.R.S. § 378-2
Statutory provision(s) providing protection from employment discrimination on the basis of gender identity	H.R.S. § 378-2[25]
Total number of employment discrimination administrative complaints filed between 2007 and 2012[26]	FY 2011-2012: 558 FY 2010-2011: 563 FY 2009-2010: 632 FY 2008-2009: 632 FY 2007-2008: 617 FY 2006-2007: 461
Total number of employment discrimination administrative complaints filed between 2007 and 2012 where at least one of the claimed bases for discrimination is sexual orientation	FY 2011-2012: 12 FY 2010-2011: 9 FY 2009-2010: 15 FY 2008-2009: 9 FY 2007-2008: 8 FY 2006-2007: 3
Total number of employment discrimination administrative complaints filed between 2007 and 2012 where at least one of the claimed bases for discrimination is gender identity	Not available[27]

ILLINOIS	
Statutory provision(s) providing protection from employment discrimination on the basis of sexual orientation	§§ 775 ILCS 5/1-103(O-1) and (Q), 5/2- 102(A), (B) and (C)
Statutory provision(s) providing protection from employment discrimination on the basis of gender identity	§§ 775 ILCS 5/1-103(O-1) and (Q), 5/2- 102(A), (B) and (C)[28]
Total number of employment discrimination dministrative complaints filed between 2007 and 2012[29]	FY 2012: 3,613 FY 2011: 3,439 FY 2010: 3,769 FY 2009: 4,007 FY 2008: 3,522 FY 2007: 3,287
Total number of employment discrimination administrative complaints filed between 2007 and 2012 where at least one of the claimed bases for discrimination is sexual orientation	FY 2012: 107 FY 2011: 133 FY 2010: 107 FY 2009: 149 FY 2008: 81 FY 2007: 103
Total number of employment discrimination administrative complaints filed between 2007 and 2012 where at least one of the claimed bases for discrimination is gender identity	Not available[30]

IOWA	
Statutory provision(s) providing protection from employment discrimination on the basis of sexual orientation	Iowa Code § 216.6
Statutory provision(s) providing protection from employment discrimination on the basis of gender identity	Iowa Code § 216.6
Total number of employment discrimination administrative complaints filed between 2007 and 2012[31]	FY 2012: 1,373 FY 2011: 1,539 FY 2010: 1,458 FY 2009: 1,644 FY 2008: 1,453 FY 2007: 1,413
Total number of employment discrimination administrative complaints filed between 2007 and 2012 where at least one of the claimed bases for discrimination is sexual orientation[32]	FY 2012: 69 FY 2011: 59 FY 2010: 93 FY 2009: 25 FY 2008: 17
Total number of employment discrimination administrative complaints filed between 2007 and 2012 where at least one of the claimed bases for discrimination is gender identity	FY 2012: 26 FY 2011: 3 FY 2010: 5 FY 2009: 3 FY 2008: 6

MAINE	
Statutory provision(s) providing protection from employment discrimination on the basis of sexual orientation	5 M.R.S. §§ 4552, and 4572 4553(9-C) and (10), 4571,
Statutory provision(s) providing protection from employment discrimination on the basis of gender identity	5 M.R.S. §§ 4552, and 4572[33] 4553(9-C) and (10), 4571,
Total number of employment discrimination administrative complaints filed between 2007 and 2012[34]	FY 2012: 542 FY 2011: 616 FY 2010: 494 FY 2009: 503 FY 2008: 623 FY 2007: 539
Total number of employment discrimination administrative complaints filed between 2007 and 2012 where at least one of the claimed bases for discrimination is sexual orientation	FY 2012: 19 FY 2011: 26 FY 2010: 34 FY 2009: 7 FY 2008: 13 FY 2007: 20
Total number of employment discrimination administrative complaints filed between 2007 and 2012 where at least one of the claimed bases for discrimination is gender identity	FY 2012: 1 FY 2011: 0 FY 2010: 0 FY 2009: 1 FY 2008: 1 FY 2007: 2

MARYLAND	
Statutory provision(s) providing protection from employment discrimination on the basis of sexual orientation	Md. Code Ann., State Gov't. §§ 20-601 – 20-609
Statutory provision(s) providing protection from employment discrimination on the basis of gender identity	None[35]
Total number of employment discrimination administrative complaints filed between 2007 and 2012[36]	FY 2012: 606 FY 2011: 480 FY 2010: 598 FY 2009: 709 FY 2008: 663 FY 2007: 645
Total number of employment discrimination administrative complaints filed between 2007 and 2012 where at least one of the claimed bases for discrimination is sexual orientation	FY 2012: 24 FY 2011: 26 FY 2010: 22 FY 2009: 23 FY 2008: 24 FY 2007: 28
Total number of employment discrimination administrative complaints filed between 2007 and 2012 where at least one of the claimed bases for discrimination is gender identity	Not available[37]

MASSACHUSETTS	
Statutory provision(s) providing protection from employment discrimination on the basis of sexual orientation	M.G.L. c. 151B, § 4(1) and (3)
Statutory provision(s) providing protection from employment discrimination on the basis of gender identity	M.G.L. c. 151B, § 4(1) and (3)[38]
Total number of employment discrimination administrative complaints filed between 2007 and 2012[39]	CY 2012: 2,654 CY 2011: 2,699 CY 2010: 2,861 CY 2009: 2,832 CY 2008: 2,947 CY 2007: 2,848
Total number of employment discrimination administrative complaints filed between 2007 and 2012 where at least one of the claimed bases for discrimination is sexual orientation	CY 2012: 105 CY 2011: 119 CY 2010: 62 CY 2009: 66 CY 2008: 73 CY 2007: 61
Total number of employment discrimination administrative complaints filed between 2007 and 2012 where at least one of the claimed bases for discrimination is gender identity	Not available[40]

MINNESOTA	
Statutory provision(s) providing protection from employment discrimination on the basis of sexual orientation	M.S.A. § 363A.08
Statutory provision(s) providing protection from employment discrimination on the basis of gender identity	M.S.A. §§ 363A.03, Subd. 44 and 363A.08[41]
Total number of employment discrimination administrative complaints filed between 2007 and 2012[42]	CY 2012: 642 CY 2011: 576 CY 2010: 612 CY 2009: 629 CY 2008: 656 CY 2007: 591
Total number of employment discrimination administrative complaints filed between 2007 and 2012 where at least one of the claimed bases for discrimination is sexual orientation	CY 2012: 28 CY 2011: 20 CY 2010: 20 CY 2009: 24 CY 2008: 24 CY 2007: 21
Total number of employment discrimination administrative complaints filed between 2007 and 2012 where at least one of the claimed bases for discrimination is gender identity	Not available[43]

NEVADA	
Statutory provision(s) providing protection from employment discrimination on the basis of sexual orientation	N.R.S. §§ 233.010 and 613.330
Statutory provision(s) providing protection from employment discrimination on the basis of gender identity	N.R.S. §§ 233.010 and 613.330[44]
Total number of employment discrimination administrative complaints filed between 2007 and 2012[45]	CY 2012: 799 CY 2011: 756 CY 2010: 544 CY 2009: 833 CY 2008: 1,014 CY 2007: 1,159
Total number of employment discrimination administrative complaints filed between 2007 and 2012 where at least one of the claimed bases for discrimination is sexual orientation	CY 2012: 47 CY 2011: 40 CY 2010: 28 CY 2009: 21 CY 2008: 44 CY 2007: 38
Total number of employment discrimination administrative complaints filed between 2007 and 2012 where at least one of the claimed bases for discrimination is gender identity[46]	CY 2012: 6 CY 2011: 0

NEW HAMPSHIRE	
Statutory provision(s) providing protection from employment discrimination on the basis of sexual orientation	N.H. R.S.A. §§ 354-A:6 and 354-A:7
Statutory provision(s) providing protection from employment discrimination on the basis of gender identity	None[47]
Total number of employment discrimination administrative complaints filed between 2007 and 2012[48]	FY 2012: 257 FY 2011: 216 FY 2010: 257 FY 2009: 208 FY 2008: 251 FY 2007: 318
Total number of employment discrimination administrative complaints filed between 2007 and 2012 where at least one of the claimed bases for discrimination is sexual orientation	FY 2012: 6 FY 2011: 11 FY 2010: 6 FY 2009: 4 FY 2008: 7 FY 2007: 14
Total number of employment discrimination administrative complaints filed between 2007 and 2012 where at least one of the claimed bases for discrimination is gender identity[49]	FY 2012: 1 FY 2011: 1

NEW JERSEY	
Statutory provision(s) providing protection from employment discrimination on the basis of sexual orientation	N.J.S.A. §§ 10:2-1, 10:5-3, 10:5-8, and 10:5-12[50] 10:5-4, 10:5-6,
Statutory provision(s) providing protection from employment discrimination on the basis of gender identity	N.J.S.A. §§ 10:2-1, 10:5-3, 10:5-8, and 10:5-12[51] 10:5-4, 10:5-6,
Total number of employment discrimination administrative complaints filed between 2007 and 2012[52]	CY 2012: 616 CY 2011: 506 CY 2010: 548 CY 2009: 505 CY 2008: 692 CY 2007: 717
Total number of employment discrimination administrative complaints filed between 2007 and 2012 where at least one of the claimed bases for discrimination is sexual orientation	CY 2012: 28 CY 2011: 20 CY 2010: 20 CY 2009: 19 CY 2008: 34 CY 2007: 39
Total number of employment discrimination administrative complaints filed between 2007 and 2012 where at least one of the claimed bases for discrimination is gender identity	CY 2012: 0 CY 2011: 3 CY 2010: 5 CY 2009: 0 CY 2008: 0 CY 2007: 0

NEW MEXICO	
Statutory provision(s) providing protection from employment discrimination on the basis of sexual orientation	N.M. Stat. Ann. § 28-1-7
Statutory provision(s) providing protection from employment discrimination on the basis of gender identity	N.M. Stat. Ann. § 28-1-7
Total number of employment discrimination administrative complaints filed between 2007 and 2012[53]	CY 2012: 479 CY 2011: 504 CY 2010: 573 CY 2009: 679 CY 2008: 690 CY 2007: 726
Total number of employment discrimination administrative complaints filed between 2007 and 2012 where at least one of the claimed bases for discrimination is sexual orientation	CY 2012: 25 CY 2011: 39 CY 2010: 41 CY 2009: 30 CY 2008: 45 CY 2007: 46
Total number of employment discrimination administrative complaints filed between 2007 and 2012 where at least one of the claimed bases for discrimination is gender identity	CY 2012: 1 CY 2011: 1 CY 2010: 3 CY 2009: 3 CY 2008: 1 CY 2007: 1

NEW YORK	
Statutory provision(s) providing protection from employment discrimination on the basis of sexual orientation	N.Y. Executive Law § 296
Statutory provision(s) providing protection from employment discrimination on the basis of gender identity	None[54]
Total number of employment discrimination administrative complaints filed between 2007 and 2012[55]	FY 2011-2012: 5,032 FY 2010-2011: 5,684 FY 2009-2010: 6,083 FY 2008-2009: 6,445 FY 2007-2008: 6,078 FY 2006-2007: 4,615
Total number of employment discrimination administrative complaints filed between 2007 and 2012 where at least one of the claimed bases for discrimination is sexual orientation	FY 2011-2012: 243 FY 2010-2011: 236 FY 2009-2010: 224 FY 2008-2009: 270 FY 2007-2008: 216 FY 2006-2007: 141
Total number of employment discrimination administrative complaints filed between 2007 and 2012 where at least one of the claimed bases for discrimination is gender identity	Not available[56]

OREGON	
Statutory provision(s) providing protection from employment discrimination on the basis of sexual orientation	ORS §§ 659A.006 and 659A.030
Statutory provision(s) providing protection from employment discrimination on the basis of gender identity	ORS §§ 174.100, 659A.006, and 659A.030[57]
Total number of employment discrimination administrative complaints filed between 2007 and 2012[58]	FY 2012: 1,676 FY 2011: 1,825 FY 2010: 1,811 FY 2009: 1,920 FY 2008: 2,009 FY 2007: 1,862 FY 2012: 30
Total number of employment discrimination administrative complaints filed between 2007 and 2012 where at least one of the claimed bases for discrimination is sexual orientation[59]	FY 2011: 35 FY 2010: 31 FY 2009: 46 FY 2008: 22 FY 2007: 32 FY 2012: 0
Total number of employment discrimination administrative complaints filed between 2007 and 2012 where at least one of the claimed bases for discrimination is gender identity	FY 2011: 6 FY 2010: 0 FY 2009: 0 FY 2008: 0 FY 2007: 0

RHODE ISLAND	
Statutory provision(s) providing protection from employment discrimination on the basis of sexual orientation	R.I. Gen. Laws §§ 28-5-3 and 28-5-7
Statutory provision(s) providing protection from employment discrimination on the basis of gender identity	R.I. Gen. Laws §§ 28-5-3 and 28-5-7[60]
Total number of employment discrimination administrative complaints filed between 2007 and 2012[61]	FY 2012: 314 FY 2011: 378 FY 2010: 382 FY 2009: 356 FY 2008: 409 FY 2007: 364
Total number of employment discrimination administrative complaints filed between 2007 and 2012 where at least one of the claimed bases for discrimination is sexual orientation	FY 2012: 8 FY 2011: 17 FY 2010: 15 FY 2009: 15 FY 2008: 15 FY 2007: 14
Total number of employment discrimination administrative complaints filed between 2007 and 2012 where at least one of the claimed bases for discrimination is gender identity	FY 2012: 2 FY 2011: 1 FY 2010: 1 FY 2009: 0 FY 2008: 0 FY 2007: 1

VERMONT	
Statutory provision(s) providing protection from employment discrimination on the basis of sexual orientation	21 V.S.A. § 495
Statutory provision(s) providing protection from employment discrimination on the basis of gender identity	21 V.S.A. § 495
Total number of employment discrimination administrative complaints filed between 2007 and 2012[62]	FY 2012: 142 FY 2011: 105 FY 2010: 105 FY 2009: 134 FY 2008: 111 FY 2007: 92
Total number of employment discrimination administrative complaints filed between 2007 and 2012 where at least one of the claimed bases for discrimination is sexual orientation	FY 2012: 4 FY 2011: 2 FY 2010: 3 FY 2009: 7 FY 2008: 4 FY 2007: 4
Total number of employment discrimination administrative complaints filed between 2007 and 2012 where at least one of the claimed bases for discrimination is gender identity	FY 2012: 1 FY 2011: 0 FY 2010: 1 FY 2009: 0 FY 2008: 1 FY 2007: 0

WASHINGTON	
Statutory provision(s) providing protection from employment discrimination on the basis of sexual orientation	Rev. Code Wash. (ARCW) §§ 49.60.030 and 49.60.180
Statutory provision(s) providing protection from employment discrimination on the basis of gender identity	Rev. Code Wash. (ARCW) §§ 49.60.030, 49.60.040(26), and 49.60.180[63]
Total number of employment discrimination administrative complaints filed between 2007 and 2012[64]	FY 2011-2012: 741 FY 2010-2011: 904 FY 2009-2010: 461 FY 2008-2009: 690 FY 2007-2008: 792 FY 2006-2007: 607
Total number of employment discrimination administrative complaints filed between 2007 and 2012 where at least one of the claimed bases for discrimination is sexual orientation	FY 2011-2012: 34 FY 2010-2011: 44 FY 2009-2010: 15 FY 2008-2009: 19 FY 2007-2008: 23 FY 2006-2007: 34
Total number of employment discrimination administrative complaints filed between 2007 and 2012 where at least one of the claimed bases for discrimination is gender identity	FY 2011-2012: 4 FY 2010-2011: 1 FY 2009-2010: 0 FY 2008-2009: 4 FY 2007-2008: 5 FY 2006-2007: 2

WISCONSIN	
Statutory provision(s) providing protection from employment discrimination on the basis of sexual orientation	Wis. Stat. §§ 111.31 and 111.36(1)(d)
Statutory provision(s) providing protection from employment discrimination on the basis of gender identity	None
Total number of employment discrimination administrative complaints filed between 2007 and 2012[65]	CY 2012: 3,383 CY 2011: 3,923 CY 2010: 3,722 CY 2009: 3,521 CY 2008: 3,847 CY 2007: 4,007
Total number of employment discrimination administrative complaints filed between 2007 and 2012 where at least one of the claimed bases for discrimination is sexual orientation	CY 2012: 69 CY 2011: 75 CY 2010: 100 CY 2009: 78 CY 2008: 66 CY 2007: 61
Total number of employment discrimination administrative complaints filed between 2007 and 2012 where at least one of the claimed bases for discrimination is gender identity	Not applicable

End Notes

[1] GAO, Sexual Orientation and Gender Identity Employment Discrimination: Overview of State Statutes and Complaint Data, GAO-10-135R (Washington, D.C.: October 1, 2009).

[2] In our 2009 report, we did not consider whether employment discrimination based on sexual orientation or gender identity may be addressed by federal case law, regulations, policy, or guidance, nor did we do so for purposes of this letter; we did note, however, that Executive

Order 13087, issued on May 28, 1998, amended Executive Order 11478 to prohibit discrimination based on sexual orientation within executive branch civilian employment.

[3] As we did in 2009, we refer to the District of Columbia as a state for purposes of this letter.

[4] The 22 states with explicit statutory provisions with regard to sexual orientation are: California, Colorado, Connecticut, Delaware, the District of Columbia, Hawaii, Illinois, Iowa, Maine, Maryland, Massachusetts, Minnesota, Nevada, New Hampshire, New Jersey, New Mexico, New York, Oregon, Rhode Island, Vermont, Washington, and Wisconsin. We did not determine whether states that lack explicit prohibitions against employment discrimination based on sexual orientation might allow such complaints to be pursued on other grounds.

[5] The 18 states with explicit statutory provisions with regard to gender identity or other similar terms, such as gender expression or transgender status, are: California, Colorado, Connecticut, Delaware, the District of Columbia, Hawaii, Illinois, Iowa, Maine, Massachusetts, Minnesota, Nevada, New Jersey, New Mexico, Oregon, Rhode Island, Vermont, and Washington. We did not determine whether any other states that lack explicit statutory provisions might allow such complaints to be pursued on other grounds, though officials in Maryland and New York, which both have statutes prohibiting employment discrimination on the basis of sexual orientation, reported in their responses to our questionnaire that individuals in their states may be able to pursue administrative complaints based on gender identity in the absence of explicit state statutory provisions. Similarly, an official in New Hampshire told us that individuals in that state have the legal right to file a charge of discrimination related to gender identity despite the absence of explicit statutory language and that such charges may be pursued under the protected categories of sex and/or mental disability, depending on jurisdictional issues.

[6] Although state case law, state regulations, or other state guidance may address issues related to employment discrimination or the scope and applicability of state employment discrimination statutes, our focus was only on the explicit language of state statutes. In addition, we did not review local government ordinances, which may also address issues related to employment discrimination.

[7] We asked states to note whether the state statutory provisions we identified were correct, incorrect, or incomplete, and to provide corrections where appropriate. We relied on the information provided by state officials and did not do additional research to identify other state statutory provisions that may be relevant to claims of employment discrimination.

[8] All states reported their complaint data to us by state fiscal year, federal fiscal year, or calendar year. Most states' fiscal years run from July 1 through June 30, and all references to a state fiscal year are to that time frame unless otherwise noted. Moreover, some states use a single year when referring to the state fiscal year and others use a 2 year designation. For instance, some states refer to "FY 2012," while other states use "FY 2011-2012" to refer to the same time period. In either case, this time period would run from July 1, 2011 through June 30, 2012. Some states reported complaint data to us by federal fiscal year, which runs from October 1 through September 30. In light of the variation in how states collect and report this information, we asked states to provide data for the most recent 7 years for which data were available to ensure that each state would provide data for the full time period included in the scope of our review, which is 2007 through 2012.

[9] In some states, the statutes prohibiting sexual orientation- or gender identity-based employment discrimination were enacted during the time period covered by our review; therefore, these states did not provide complaint data for the full time period requested. In addition, seven states that have explicit statutory prohibitions against gender identity- based employment discrimination reported that, during the time period covered by our review, they did not

separately track data related to the number of gender identity-based complaints they received. These states are: California, Connecticut, Delaware, Hawaii, Illinois, Massachusetts, and Minnesota.

[10] The relevant protected classes explicitly identified in state statute are "gender identity" and "gender expression."

[11] All complaint data in this table are reported by calendar year.

[12] According to a state official, California does not separately track complaints filed on the basis of gender identity. Currently, complaints filed on the basis of gender identity are tracked with complaints filed on the basis of sex.

[13] State statute prohibits employment discrimination on the basis of sexual orientation, which is defined to include, in relevant part, "transgender status."

[14] All complaint data in this table are reported by state fiscal year.

[15] A state official told us that sexual orientation and transgender status were not protected statuses under Colorado statute before FY 2007-2008.

[16] The relevant protected class explicitly identified in state statute is "gender identity or expression." This became a protected class status on October 1, 2011.

[17] Connecticut began tracking employment discrimination complaint data by calendar year rather than state fiscal year in 2010. A state official acknowledged that this may have resulted in some double counting of complaints for calendar year 2010.

[18] A state official reported that the state does not separately track complaints based on gender identity.

[19] Delaware amended its employment discrimination statute in June 2013 to add gender identity to the list of protected categories.

[20] All complaint data in this table are reported by federal fiscal year.

[21] As we reported in 2009, sexual orientation became a protected status for purposes of employment discrimination on July 1, 2009. As a result, FY 2010 is the first year for which the state has data for this category.

[22] According to a state official, the numbers listed for complaints based on sexual orientation may include complaints based on gender identity; the state does not separately track the number of complaints filed on the basis of this category.

[23] The relevant protected class explicitly identified in state statute is "gender identity or expression."

[24] All complaint data in this table are reported by state fiscal year, which runs from October 1 through September 30.

[25] Hawaii amended its statute in 2011 to clarify existing law with regard to sex discrimination and provide that discrimination based upon "gender identity or expression" constitutes a form of sex discrimination.

[26] All complaint data in this table are reported by state fiscal year.

[27] Hawaii reported that it does not compile separate statistics for gender identity complaints, which it categorizes as sex discrimination complaints.

[28] State statute prohibits employment discrimination on the basis of sexual orientation, which is defined to include, in relevant part, "gender-related identity, whether or not traditionally associated with the person's designated sex at birth."

[29] All complaint data in this table are reported by state fiscal year.

[30] According to a state official, complaints based on gender identity are included in the numbers of complaints based on sexual orientation.

[31] All complaint data in this table are reported by state fiscal year.

[32] As we reported in 2009, Iowa started accepting employment discrimination complaints on the bases of sexual orientation and gender identity on July 1, 2007. As a result, Iowa did not report data for FY 2007 on these bases.

[33] State statute prohibits employment discrimination on the basis of sexual orientation, which is defined to include, in relevant part, "gender identity or expression."

[34] All complaint data in this table are reported by state fiscal year.

[35] Although gender identity is not explicitly identified as a protected category under state statute, a state official reported that Maryland accepts gender identity complaints under the category of sex.

[36] All complaint data in this table are reported by state fiscal year.

[37] Maryland reported that it does not separately track gender identity complaints.

[38] Massachusetts added gender identity as a protected category in November 2011, effective July 2012.

[39] All complaint data in this table are reported by calendar year.

[40] According to a state official, before Massachusetts explicitly added gender identity as a protected category, effective July 2012, the state accepted complaints alleging gender identity employment discrimination under the categories of disability, gender, or sexual orientation, and gender identity complaints previously filed under these other bases were not tracked separately. Although the state has been accepting complaints under the new protected category of gender identity since July 2012, this official stated that Massachusetts had not been specifically tracking gender identity complaints since that date, but has now begun doing so.

[41] State statute prohibits employment discrimination on the basis of sexual orientation, which is defined to include, in relevant part, "having or being perceived as having a self-image or identity not traditionally associated with one's biological maleness or femaleness."

[42] All complaint data in this table are reported by calendar year.

[43] According to a state official, the numbers listed above for sexual orientation administrative complaints include all gender identity administrative complaints.

[44] The relevant protected category explicitly identified in state statute is "gender identity or expression." This became a protected category on October 1, 2011.

[45] All complaint data in this table are reported by calendar year.

[46] Because this became a protected category on October 1, 2011, data from earlier years are not available.

[47] Although gender identity is not explicitly identified as a protected category under state statute, a state official reported that individuals have the legal right to file a charge of discrimination related to gender identity and that such charges may be pursued under the protected categories of sex and/or mental disability, depending on jurisdictional issues.

[48] All complaint data in this table are reported by federal fiscal year.

[49] A state official reported that the state currently does not track gender identity complaints separately from other gender discrimination complaints, but the state official reviewed complaints for FYs 2011 and 2012 and determined that there was one complaint related to gender identity in each of those years. The official noted further that the state will separately track information related to complaints involving transgendered persons in the future.

[50] The relevant protected class explicitly identified in state statute is "affectional or sexual orientation."

[51] The relevant protected class explicitly identified in state statute is "gender identity or expression."

[52] All complaint data in this table are reported by calendar year.

[53] All complaint data in this table are reported by calendar year.

[54] Although gender identity is not explicitly identified as a protected category under state employment discrimination statutes, a state official reported that the state investigates some gender identity cases under the protected categories of disability and/or sex.

[55] All complaint data in this table are reported by state fiscal year, which runs from April 1 through March 31.

[56] A state official reported that the state does not separately track gender identity cases investigated on the bases of disability and/or sex.

[57] State statute prohibits employment discrimination on the basis of sexual orientation, which is defined to include, in relevant part, "an individual's...gender identity, regardless of whether the individual's gender identity, appearance, expression, or behavior differs from that traditionally associated with the individual's sex at birth."

[58] All complaint data in this table are reported by state fiscal year.

[59] A state official reported that Oregon's statute prohibiting employment discrimination on the basis of sexual orientation and gender identity took effect in January 2008, and the state investigated sexual orientation and gender identity discrimination claims under some city and county ordinances before that time. Data for FY 2007 include complaints pursued under city and county ordinances only, while data for FY 2008 include sexual orientation and gender identity discrimination complaints pursued under city and county ordinances and state law. Data for FY 2009 through FY 2012 include only complaints pursued under state law.

[60] The relevant protected class explicitly identified in state statute is "gender identity or expression."

[61] All complaint data in this table are reported by state fiscal year.

[62] All complaint data in this table are reported by federal fiscal year.

[63] State statute prohibits employment discrimination on the basis of sexual orientation, which is defined to include, in relevant part, "gender expression or identity." "Gender expression or identity" is defined to mean "having or being perceived as having a gender identity, self-image, appearance, behavior, or expression, whether or not that gender identity, self-image, appearance, behavior, or expression is different from that traditionally associated with the sex assigned to that person at birth."

[64] All complaint data in this table are reported by state fiscal year.

[65] All complaint data in this table are reported by calendar year.

In: Federal Employees and Sexual Orientation ISBN: 978-1-63484-376-8
Editor: Ross Henderson

Chapter 3

SEXUAL ORIENTATION AND GENDER IDENTITY DISCRIMINATION IN EMPLOYMENT: A LEGAL ANALYSIS OF THE EMPLOYMENT NON-DISCRIMINATION ACT (ENDA)*

Jody Feder and Cynthia Brougher

SUMMARY

Introduced in various incarnations in every congressional session since the 103rd Congress, the proposed Employment Non-Discrimination Act (ENDA; H.R. 1755/S. 815) would prohibit discrimination based on an individual's actual or perceived sexual orientation or gender identity by public and private employers in hiring, discharge, compensation, and other terms and conditions of employment. The stated purpose of the legislation is "to address the history and persistent, widespread pattern of discrimination, including unconstitutional discrimination, on the basis of sexual orientation and gender identity by private sector employers and local, State, and Federal Government employers," as well as to provide effective remedies for such discrimination. Patterned on Title VII of the

---

* This is an edited, reformatted and augmented version of a Congressional Research Service publication R40934, prepared for Members and Committees of Congress, dated July 15, 2013.

Civil Rights Act of 1964, the act would be enforced by the Equal Employment Opportunity Commission (EEOC).

INTRODUCTION

Introduced in various incarnations in every congressional session since the 103rd Congress, the proposed Employment Non-Discrimination Act (ENDA; H.R. 1755/S. 815) would prohibit discrimination based on an individual's actual or perceived sexual orientation or gender identity by public and private employers in hiring, discharge, compensation, and other terms and conditions of employment. The stated purpose of the legislation is "to address the history and persistent, widespread pattern of discrimination, including unconstitutional discrimination, on the basis of sexual orientation and gender identity by private sector employers and local, State, and Federal Government employers," as well as to provide effective remedies for such discrimination.[1]

Specific exemptions from coverage are included for religious organizations and educational institutions, the armed services, and employers with fewer than 15 employees. Preferential treatment or quotas on the basis of sexual orientation or gender identity and "disparate impact" claims of discrimination would be specifically precluded. Patterned on Title VII of the Civil Rights Act of 1964,[2] the act would be enforced by the Equal Employment Opportunity Commission (EEOC).

Although earlier versions of the legislation, dating back to 1975, proposed simply amending the provisions of Title VII to add "sexual orientation" to categories of discrimination already prohibited, more recent versions of ENDA have proposed a stand-alone legislative safeguard against sexual orientation and gender identity discrimination in employment. Because the proposed legislation incorporates by reference many of Title VII's provisions, it is similar in scope to the earlier law. However, because discrimination on the basis of sexual orientation and gender identity was not before Congress when it enacted Title VII, the measures also differ in several significant respects.

On July 10, 2013, the Senate Committee on Health, Education, Labor, and Pensions passed an amended version of ENDA. The differences between ENDA as introduced and as amended during markup in the Senate are described in more detail below.

Coverage

Like Title VII, ENDA would prohibit employers, employment agencies, and labor organizations from discriminating on the basis of sexual orientation or gender identity. Both public and private employers would be covered, although private employers who have fewer than 15 employees would be exempt. Like Title VII, ENDA would define "employer" to exclude "bona fide private membership" clubs that qualify for federal tax exemptions. As described in greater detail below, religious organizations and the Armed Forces would also be specifically excluded from coverage under the legislation.

Likewise, most public and private employees would be protected by ENDA, including employees covered by the Government Employee Rights Act of 1991 and the Congressional Accountability Act of 1995.[3] Volunteers who receive no compensation, however, would not be covered under the legislation.

Prohibited Acts

If enacted, ENDA would make it an unlawful employment practice for an employer to discriminate against an individual "because of such individual's actual or perceived sexual orientation or gender identity."[4] The legislation's delineation of prohibited employment practices substantially tracks the catalogue of employer malfeasance condemned by Title VII, which generally makes it unlawful for employers with 15 or more employees, employment agencies, and labor organizations to discriminate against employees or applicants for employment because of race, color, religion, sex, or national origin.[5] Thus, all forms of employment and preemployment bias would be forbidden, including discrimination in hiring, discharge, promotion, layoff and recall, compensation and fringe benefits, classification, training, apprenticeship, referral, union membership, and other "terms, conditions, or privileges of employment." Likewise, employers would not be allowed to "limit, segregate, or classify" employees in ways that "deprive or tend to deprive" them of job opportunities or "adversely affect" their employment status. A comparable range of employment agency and labor organization practices, again largely borrowed from Title VII, would be prohibited by ENDA, which also would prohibit discrimination in apprenticeship or training programs. In addition, the legislation incorporates Title VII language that would specifically prohibit retaliation against employees who complain of discriminatory conduct.

Despite these similarities with respect to prohibited acts, ENDA would differ from Title VII in several significant ways. For example, one provision without direct parallel in Title VII's statutory text would make an employer liable for employment actions that are "based on the sexual orientation or gender identity of a person with whom the individual associates or has associated."[6] Another provision would narrow the evidentiary options available in sexual orientation and gender identity cases by stipulating that employees may bring only disparate treatment claims, meaning that disparate impact claims would be prohibited. Disparate treatment generally occurs when an employer intentionally discriminates against an employee by treating a similarly situated employee differently, while disparate impact occurs when an employer's acts or policies are facially neutral but have an adverse effect on a class of employees and are not otherwise reasonable. Proof of intent to discriminate is required to prove a disparate treatment claim, but is not required to establish a disparate impact claim, which can often be proved through the use of statistics. Because disparate impact claims would not be allowed under ENDA, a plaintiff would have to prove that an employer intended to discriminate, a higher evidentiary threshold. Reinforcing this limitation is another provision that would bar the EEOC from requiring employers to collect or provide statistics on sexual orientation and gender identity.

However, nothing in ENDA would prohibit employers from voluntarily submitting such statistics to the EEOC.

In addition to these provisions, the ENDA legislation would clarify that preferential treatment or quotas on the basis of sexual orientation or gender identity would not be required. Likewise, employers would not be prohibited from requiring employees to adhere to reasonable dress or grooming standards, as long as the employer permits employees who have undergone gender transition to comply with the same dress or grooming standards for the gender to which the employee has transitioned or is transitioning. Finally, ENDA states that nothing in the act should be construed to require construction of new or additional facilities.

As noted above, the Senate version of ENDA was recently amended during markup in the Committee on Health, Education, Labor, and Pensions. The amended bill contains several additional requirements, including a provision that would bar individuals who sue under both ENDA and Title VII from being awarded remedies under both statutes,[7] as well as a section that would authorize mixed-motive claims, which generally involve employment actions that are based on both permissible and impermissible reasons.[8] In addition, the committee-approved version of ENDA would revise the bill's attorney's fees provisions (discussed below) by clarifying that authority to award such fees would be limited "to the same extent as is permitted under Title VII...."[9]

Sexual Orientation

As noted above, ENDA would prohibit employment discrimination on the basis of actual or perceived sexual orientation. "Sexual orientation" would be defined to mean "homosexuality, heterosexuality, or bisexuality."[10] In contrast, Title VII's prohibition against discrimination on the basis of sex has consistently been interpreted to exclude discrimination on the basis of sexual orientation. Although some have argued that sex discrimination encompasses sexual orientation discrimination, the courts have generally rejected that theory, reasoning that the prohibition against sex discrimination refers only to the traditional definition of biological sex.[11] Because Title VII does not protect against employment discrimination on the basis of sexual orientation, ENDA would significantly expand the scope of protection under current employment discrimination law.

It is important to note, however, that courts have held that the fact that a victim of discrimination is gay or bisexual does not preclude a claim under Title VII. For example, in some cases, courts have allowed Title VII claims to proceed when an individual who is gay can demonstrate that he or she was the victim of unlawful sex discrimination in the form of sexual harassment or gender stereotyping.

In the context of sexual harassment, recent court decisions have been guided by the Supreme Court's decision in *Oncale v. Sundowner Offshore Services*.[12] In that case, a male employee suffered physical abuse of a sexual nature, but his claims of sexual harassment were initially denied because the lower court held that same-sex sexual harassment is not actionable under Title VII. The Supreme Court reversed, holding that, in cases of alleged sexual harassment, the gender of the victim and harasser are not dispositive, but rather the critical question is whether the harassment occurred "because of sex."[13] The Court also recognized that an inference that harassment is "because of sex" is not obvious where the harasser and the victim are of the same sex, but provided three examples of how such an inference could be established: (1) if the harasser sexually desired the victim; (2) if the harasser was hostile to the presence of one sex in the workplace; or (3) if comparative data showed that the harasser targeted only members of one sex.[14]

Based upon the Supreme Court's opinion in *Price Waterhouse v. Hopkins*,[15] individuals who are gay may also prevail under Title VII when an employer discriminates based on the employee's failure to conform to sex stereotypes. In *Price Waterhouse*, a female employee was denied partnership in an accounting firm, despite the fact that she was regarded as a high performer.[16] Furthermore, partners in the firm had instructed her to act more femininely in order to be considered for a partnership in the future.[17] The Court held that Price Waterhouse was applying standards for partnership in a prohibited sexually disparate manner, in that Title VII did not permit an employer to evaluate female employees based upon their conformity with the employer's stereotypical view of femininity.[18] As a result, harassment of an individual for failure to conform to sex stereotypes could constitute harassment "because of sex," even if the animosity towards nonconformance is caused by a belief that such behavior indicates homosexuality.

Based on these decisions, it appears that individuals who are gay may currently be protected under Title VII if they are discriminated against because of sex. However, such individuals would not be protected by current law if they were the victim of discrimination on the basis of sexual orientation, a situation that ENDA appears designed to remedy. It is important to note that ENDA states that the act should not be construed to invalidate or limit rights under any other federal or state law. Therefore, ENDA would not appear to alter the current protections that may be available to individuals who are gay under Title VII or state law.

Gender Identity

ENDA would also prohibit employment discrimination on the basis of actual or perceived gender identity. "Gender identity" would be defined to mean "the gender-related identity, appearance, or mannerisms or other gender-related characteristics of an individual, with or without regard to the individual's designated sex at birth." Under current law, Title VII does not expressly prohibit gender identity discrimination. Nonetheless, there have been cases interpreting Title VII's prohibition against sex discrimination to cover gender and/or gender identity. Although the majority of federal courts to consider the issue have concluded that discrimination on the basis of gender identity is not sex discrimination,[19] there have been several courts that have reached the opposite conclusion in the years since the Supreme Court's decision in *Price Waterhouse*. As noted above, the *Price Waterhouse* decision, in which the Court repeatedly declared that Title VII bars discrimination on the basis of "gender," held that discrimination against a female employee who did not conform to socially constructed gender expectations constituted unlawful gender discrimination in violation of Title VII. Since *Price Waterhouse*, several courts have openly speculated that the *Price Waterhouse* decision "seem[s] to indicate that the word 'sex' in Title VII encompasses both gender and sex, and forbids discrimination because of one's failure to act in a way expected of a man or a woman."[20]

For example, in *Smith v. Salem*, a male firefighter who was undergoing gender transition to female argued that he had been suspended because of his feminine appearance.[21] The U.S. Court of Appeals for the Sixth Circuit held that, to the extent that the firefighter asserted that she experienced discriminatory treatment due to the fact that she did not conform to what her employer believed males should look and act like, she had sufficiently plead a prima facie case of sex discrimination.[22] Similarly, in *Barnes v. Cincinnati*, a male police officer undergoing gender transition to female was denied a promotion because she acted too femininely in her supervisors' opinions.[23]

More recently, the EEOC adopted a similar interpretation of Title VII. In *Macy v. Holder*,[24] a job applicant alleged that she had been hired for a position in the Bureau of Alcohol, Tobacco, Firearms and Explosives but was subsequently denied the job when she informed the agency that she was undergoing a gender transition. The EEOC ruled that intentional discrimination based on gender identity is sex discrimination and therefore permitted the complainant's Title VII claim to proceed. Although this administrative decision is not binding on the federal courts, it could have a significant enforcement effect, given that the EEOC is responsible for handling initial claims processing for employment discrimination complaints.

Meanwhile, the U.S. Court of Appeals for the Eleventh Circuit reached a similar conclusion on constitutional grounds in a case involving a Georgia state employee who was fired from her job for being transgender. According to the court, "[w]e conclude that a government agent violates the Equal Protection Clause's prohibition of sex-based discrimination when he or she fires a transgender or transsexual employee because of his or her gender non-conformity."[25]

Although some courts have held that Title VII's prohibition against sex discrimination may encompass claims based on gender identity when unlawful gender stereotyping is involved, the courts have not recognized gender identity discrimination on its own to be an unlawful employment practice under Title VII. As a result, ENDA would expand the scope of protection under current employment law by explicitly prohibiting gender identity discrimination. As noted above, ENDA states that the act should not be construed to invalidate or limit rights under any other federal or state law. Therefore, ENDA would not appear to alter the current protections based on gender identity that may be available under Title VII or state law.

Exceptions for the Armed Forces and Religious Organizations

ENDA contains several exceptions. First, the Armed Forces, which include the Army, Navy, Air Force, Marines, and Coast Guard, would be exempt, and the legislation specifies that current laws regarding veterans' preferences in employment would not be affected. The courts have similarly held that uniformed military personnel are not covered by Title VII,[26] although civilian military employees are protected by Title VII.[27]

Notably, certain religious organizations would also be exempt from coverage under ENDA. This exemption is consistent with previous congressional efforts to avoid infringing on a religious organization's exercise of religion with respect to its employment practices, such as the Title VII provision that exempts certain religious organizations from compliance with that statute. In that sense, ENDA would expand the current protection offered to religious organizations relating to discrimination in employment practices.

Title VII includes two exceptions that allow certain employers to consider religion in employment decisions. Specifically, the prohibition against religious discrimination does not apply to "a religious corporation, association, educational institution, or society with respect to the employment of individuals of a particular religion to perform work connected with the carrying on by such corporation, association, educational institution, or society of its activities."[28] The prohibition also does not apply to religious educational institutions if the institution "is, in whole or in substantial part, owned, supported, controlled, or managed by a particular religion or by a particular [organization], or if the curriculum of the [institution] is directed toward the propagation of a particular religion."[29] These exemptions are sometimes referred to as sections 702(a) and 703(e)(2), respectively. The Title VII exemptions apply with respect to discrimination based on religion only and do not allow qualifying organizations to discriminate on any other basis forbidden by Title VII, such as race, color, national origin, or sex.[30]

Like Title VII, ENDA "shall not apply to a corporation, association, educational institution or institution of learning, or society that is exempt from the religious discrimination provisions of title VII of the Civil Rights Act of 1964 pursuant to section 702(a) or 703(e)(2) of such Act."[31] By exempting the organizations covered by the 702(a) and 703(e)(2) exemptions of Title VII, ENDA ensures that such organizations would not be required to hire or retain an individual if the organization had objections to the individual's sexual orientation or gender identity. Notably, the language of Title VII does not appear to require that the organization's religious beliefs oppose certain sexual orientations or gender identifications. In other words, the ENDA exemption does not appear to limit the permissibility of religious organizations' discrimination based on sexual orientation or gender identity to instances in which those factors may conflict with religious beliefs. For example, under the legislation, even religious organizations whose religious teachings do not oppose homosexuality could be permitted to refuse to hire a gay applicant. Thus, the proposed legislation likely would not interfere with religious organizations' employment practices involving considerations of sexual orientation or gender identity of employees and applicants. To the contrary, it may actually broaden these organizations' ability to discriminate in hiring. In this sense, the ENDA exception goes farther than the Title VII exception, which allows religious employers to discriminate on the basis of religion but not on the basis of race, color, national origin, or sex.

The question of what organizations would be covered by the ENDA exemption may be resolved by looking at organizations that have sought protection under the relevant Title VII exemptions. Title VII did not define what organizations would qualify for an exemption under the statute, and court decisions have indicated several factors relevant to deciding whether an organization qualifies, including (1) the purpose or mission of the organization; (2) the ownership, affiliation, or source of financial support of the organization; (3) requirements placed upon staff and members of the organization (faculty and students if the organization is a school); and (4) the extent of religious practices in or the religious nature of products and services offered by the organization.[32] No single factor appears to be dispositive and as one federal court has noted, "the decision whether an organization is 'religious' for purposes of the exemption cannot be based on its conformity to some preconceived notion of what a religious organization should do, but must be measured with reference to the particular religion identified by the organization."[33]

Organizations may qualify for an exemption if their purpose, character, and operations incorporate elements of their religion. For example, in *LeBoon v. Lancaster Jewish Community Center Association*, a Jewish community center qualified for an exemption under Title VII when it terminated the employment of a Christian employee.[34] The center's stated mission was to promote Jewish life and values, and three local rabbis were significantly involved in its management. Furthermore, the center conducted a variety of programs observing Jewish religious holidays and traditions. The U.S. Court of Appeals for the Third Circuit noted the organization's primarily religious character, indicated by factors such as the composition of its administrative body and the programs that it offered to the community. Ultimately, the court held that religious organizations may qualify for an exemption despite engaging in secular activities, not adhering to the strictest tenets of the religion, or not hiring only co-religionists.[35]

On the other hand, courts have declined to apply the exemption to organizations that cannot demonstrate a connection between religious beliefs and the organization itself. In *Equal Employment Opportunity Commission (EEOC) v. Townley Engineering and Manufacturing Company*, the owners of a mining equipment manufacturing company claimed an exemption under Title VII after an employee initiated legal proceedings objecting to attending mandatory religious services.[36] The owners claimed that they founded their company under "a covenant with God that their business would be a Christian, faith-operated business" and that they were "unable to separate God from any portion of their daily lives, including their activities at the Townley company."[37] The court reviewed legal precedent and the legislative history of Title VII and held that the central function of the exemption "has been to exempt churches, synagogues, and the like, and organizations closely affiliated with those entities."[38] It noted that Townley was a for-profit company, producing a secular product, with no affiliation with or support from a church. Further, it had no religious purpose. Although the court recognized that the owners did include religious characteristics in their operation of their company, the court held that "the beliefs of the owners and operators of a corporation are not simply enough in themselves to make the corporation 'religious'" under the Title VII exemption.[39]

In *Pime v. Loyola University of Chicago*, a former Jesuit university sought to retain its religious identity even after it had evolved into a secular institution.[40] It claimed an exemption under Title VII as a university supported, controlled, or managed in whole or in part by a religious society because it reserved three tenured positions for Jesuits and several university administrators (including the president, one-third of the trustees, and other officers) were also Jesuits. However, the Society of Jesus did not instruct the president or trustees with regard to university matters and did not control the decisions of other Jesuits who served in official positions at the university.[41] As a result, the U.S. Court of Appeals for the Seventh Circuit held that, despite a "Jesuit presence" on campus, the university did not qualify for an exemption from Title VII.[42]

In a similar case, *EEOC v. Kamehameha Schools/Bishop Estate*, the U.S. Court of Appeals for the Ninth Circuit likewise held that a school that hired Protestant teachers to provide a secular education to students did not qualify for an exemption under Title VII.[43] The Kamehameha Schools were created by the will of a member of the Hawaiian royal family, which provided that teachers be members of the Protestant faith and claimed an exemption as a religious educational institution based on this provision. However, the court held that the schools' purpose and character were primarily secular and not religious, noting that the religious characteristics the schools had (i.e., comparative religious studies, scheduled prayers and services, Bible quotations in a school publication, and employment of nominally Protestant teachers) were common to private schools. The court also noted that the schools had embraced a broad mandate to help native Hawaiians "participate in contemporary society for a rewarding and productive life" through a solid secular education.[44] As a result, the court held that the teachers' religious affiliation was an insufficient basis to qualify for an exemption as a religious institution.

The result in *Kamehameha Schools* was influenced to some degree by the absence of church ownership or control. Indeed, the court of appeals observed that it had found "no case holding the Title VII exemption to be applicable where the institution was not wholly or partially owned by a church."[45] Subsequently, in *Killinger v. Samford University*,[46] the U.S. Court of Appeals for the Eleventh Circuit held that a Baptist college was an exempt religious institution which could require professors to subscribe to the school's religious doctrine. The court noted that a Baptist convention comprised the largest single source of revenue for the college and that the school's charter listed as its chief purpose the "promotion of Christian Religion." Thus, under Title VII precedent, independent Christian and other religious schools not owned, financed, or controlled by church bodies may find it difficult to qualify for the "religious organization" exemption in ENDA. Of course, as stand-alone legislation, it is possible that courts would find that the policy concerns underlying ENDA are sufficiently different from Title VII to warrant a less restrictive reading of the former. Absent clarification in ENDA itself, or its legislative history, any resolution of the issue would have to await further judicial elaboration.

ENFORCEMENT AND REMEDIES

Enforcement procedures under ENDA would parallel the enforcement provisions of Title VII. Thus, the Department of Justice (DOJ) would enforce ENDA against state and local governments, and administrative enforcement with respect to private employment would be delegated to the EEOC, which would have the same authority to receive and investigate complaints, to negotiate voluntary settlements, and to seek judicial remedies as it currently exercises under Title VII. Similarly, in devising remedies for sexual orientation or gender identity discrimination under the legislation, a federal court would have the same jurisdiction and powers as the court has to enforce Title VII. In general, federal courts possess broad remedial discretion under Title VII, including the ability to enjoin the unlawful employment practice and to "order such affirmative action as may be appropriate, which may include, but is not limited to, reinstatement or hiring of employees, with or without back pay ... or any other relief as the court deems appropriate."[47] Although the Supreme Court early on adopted a "make-whole" theory of Title VII relief,[48] including use of affirmative action remedies, minority preferences and the like, where necessary to redress discrimination of a particularly "egregious" or "longstanding" nature, ENDA would specifically forbid employers from using quotas or preferential treatment.

Likewise, the remedies under ENDA would be patterned on Title VII's remedial provisions. Under Title VII, victims of discrimination may seek equitable relief, including limited back pay awards for wage, salary, and fringe benefits lost as the result of discrimination. Private employers who intentionally discriminate in violation of the statute may be liable for compensatory and punitive damages, while plaintiffs may seek awards of compensatory, but not punitive, damages against federal, state, and local governmental agencies. The following ceilings or "caps" are established by law for compensatory and punitive damages combined: (1) $50,000 for defendants who have 15 to 100 employees; (2) $100,000 for employers with 101 to 200 employees; (3) $200,000 for employers with 201 to 500 employees; and (4) $300,000 for employers with more than 500 employees.[49] The Supreme Court has also excluded from the statutory limits on damages so-called "front pay," awarded to redress discrimination victims for continuing injury in promotion or discharge cases where reinstatement is not a feasible remedy.[50] These Title VII remedies appear to be applicable to claims that would be filed under ENDA.

Meanwhile, ENDA would waive the states' Eleventh Amendment immunity from suit for sexual orientation discrimination or gender identity against employees or applicants within any state "program or activity" that receives federal financial assistance. The Eleventh Amendment provides states with immunity from claims brought under federal law in both federal and state courts.[51] Although Congress may waive the states' sovereign immunity by "appropriate" legislation enacted pursuant to §5 of the Fourteenth Amendment,[52] the scope of congressional power to create a private right of action against the states for monetary damages has been substantially narrowed by a series of Supreme Court decisions.

The era of a reinvigorated Eleventh Amendment immunity can be traced to *Seminole Tribe v. Florida*,[53] which invalidated a portion of the Indian Gaming Regulatory Act authorizing tribal suits against the states. Neither the Commerce Clause nor Section 5 proved to be an effective vehicle to override state sovereign immunity. Three years later, in *Alden v. Maine*[54] the Supreme Court ruled that the states could not be sued, even in their own courts, for violation of the Fair Labor Standards Act. *City of Boerne v. Flores*[55] announced the Court's new framework for determining the validity of congressional action under Section 5. In holding unconstitutional the Religious Freedom Restoration Act, Justice Kennedy wrote that Congress's Section 5 power was remedial only; it was not a basis for legislation defining the substantive content of the equal protection guarantee. Moreover, the remedy had to be "congruent and proportional" to the scope and frequency of any violations identified by Congress. These constitutional limitations were subsequently applied by the Court to hold the states immune from private lawsuits under the Age Discrimination in Employment Act,[56] the Violence Against Women Act,[57] and the Americans with Disabilities Act.[58]

Taken together, these decisions restrict the ability of private individuals to take the states to court for federal civil rights violations. They may not, however, apply to states' voluntary acceptance of federal benefits that are expressly conditioned on waiver of Eleventh Amendment immunity. "Congress may, in the exercise of its spending power, condition its grant of funds to the States upon their taking certain actions that Congress could not require them to take, and that acceptance of the funds entails an agreement to the actions."[59] Thus, when a statute enacted under the Spending Clause[60] conditions grants to the states upon an unambiguous waiver of Eleventh Amendment immunity, as ENDA proposes, "the condition is constitutionally permissible as long as it rests on the state's voluntary and knowing acceptance of it."[61]

Finally, the attorney's fees provision in ENDA differs somewhat from the attorney's fees provision in Title VII. Under Title VII, a court is generally authorized to award "reasonable" attorney's fees (including expert fees) to a "prevailing" plaintiff, unless special circumstances make such an award unjust.[62] Complainants may be considered "prevailing parties" if "they succeed on any significant issue in litigation which achieves some of the benefit the parties sought in bringing the suit."[63] Although either a plaintiff or a defendant may be the prevailing party, fee awards to defendant employers are not the general rule, given the public interest in having Title VII plaintiffs act as "private attorneys general" and the likelihood that defendant employers would have less need of financial assistance.[64] In addition, in cases involving federal employment, both the EEOC and federal agencies are authorized to award reasonable attorney's fees or costs.[65] The EEOC, however, does not appear to have such authority with respect to private sector employment discrimination claims.

Under ENDA, courts would have the same authority to award attorney's fees to prevailing parties as they do under Title VII. ENDA would similarly authorize the EEOC to award such fees, but, unlike Title VII, ENDA would appear to allow the EEOC to make such awards in cases involving both federal and private employment discrimination claims.

End Notes

[1] H.R. 1755/S. 815, §2, 113th Cong.

[2] 42 U.S.C. §§2000e et seq.

[3] Id. at §2000e-16; 2 U.S.C. §1301.

[4] H.R. 1755/S. 815, §4, 113th Cong.

[5] 42 U.S.C. §2000e-2.

[6] It is important to note that the scope of legal protection afforded persons based on their "perceived" orientation may be difficult to gauge. There is no comparable language in Title VII prohibiting discrimination on the basis of "perceived" characteristics applicable to discrimination prohibited by the statute. Thus, courts would apparently be left the task of developing appropriate standards of proof in such "perceived" orientation cases.

[7] S. 815, §10(d).

[8] S. 815, §4(h). Despite this change, the amended bill does not appear to adopt similar language regarding mixed-motive claims in its anti-retaliation section. This may make proving causation in retaliation cases brought under the bill more difficult in light of the recently issued U.S. Supreme Court opinion in University of Texas Southwestern Medical Center v. Nassar, No. 12-484, 2013 U.S. LEXIS 4704 (2013). In Nassar, the Court held that the retaliation provision of Title VII requires a plaintiff to prove "but-for" causation. Id. at *23-24. In other words, an employee cannot successfully sue for retaliation if an employer can demonstrate that there was another, non-retaliatory factor motivating its decision. The Court's analysis in Nassar applied an earlier analysis concerning near identical language in the Age Discrimination in Employment Act. Id. at *20-23 (citing Gross v. FBL Fin. Servs, Inc., 557 U. S. 167, 178 (2009)). The Court's decision may therefore restrict the ability of employees to bring retaliation claims under ENDA.

[9] S. 815, §12(b).

[10] The legislation does not define these terms, although the terms were formerly defined elsewhere in the U.S. Code in the context of the military's now-repealed "Don't Ask, Don't Tell" policy. 10 U.S.C. §654(f) (2007). Among the states that do prohibit discrimination on the basis of sexual orientation, it is almost universally defined as including homosexuality, bisexuality, or heterosexuality. See Government Accounting Office, Sexual Orientation-Based Employment Discrimination: States' Experience with Statutory Prohibitions at 2-4, tbl.1, July 9, 2002, available at http://www.gao.gov/new.items/d02878r.pdf.

[11] See, e.g., Spearman v. Ford Motor Co., 231 F.3d 1080 (7th Cir. 2000); Higgins v. New Balance Ath. Shoe, Inc., 194 F.3d 252 (1st Cir. 1999); Williamson v. A.G. Edwards & Sons, Inc., 876 F.2d 69 (8th Cir. 1989); DeSantis v. Pacific Tel. and Tel. Co., 608 F.2d 327 (9th Cir. 1979); Smith v. Liberty Mut. Ins. Co., 569 F.2d 325 (5th Cir. 1978).

[12] 523 U.S. 75 (1998).

[13] Id. at 77, 81.

[14] Id. at 80-81.

[15] 490 U.S. 228 (1989).

[16] Id. at 233-234.

[17] Id. at 235.

[18] Id. at 250-251.

[19] See, e.g., Ulane v. Eastern Airlines, 742 F.2d 1081 (7th Cir. 1984); Sommers v. Budget Mktg., Inc., 667 F.2d 748, 750 (8th Cir.1982); Holloway v. Arthur Andersen, 566 F.2d 659 (9th Cir. 1977); Etsitty v. Utah Transit Auth., 502 F.3d 1215 (10th Cir. 2007).

[20] Enriquez v. West Jersey Health Sys., 342 N.J. Super. 501, 512 (App. Div. 2001) (holding that a New Jersey state law barring sex discrimination in employment includes gender discrimination and thus protects transsexuals). See also, Smith v. City of Salem, 378 F.3d 566 (6th Cir. 2004); Schwenk v. Hartford, 204 F.3d 1187, 1201-02 (9th Cir. 2000); Schroer v. Billington, 424 F. Supp. 2d 203 (D.D.C. 2006).

[21] 378 F.3d 566 (6th Cir. 2004).

[22] Id. at 575.

[23] 401 F.3d 729 (6th Cir. 2005).

[24] Macy v. Holder, EEOC Appeal No. 0120120821 (April 23, 2012).

[25] Glenn v. Brumby, 663 F.3d 1312, 1320 (11th Cir. 2011).

[26] See, e.g., Luckett v. Bure, 290 F.3d 493 (2d Cir. 2002).

[27] 42 U.S.C. §2000e-16(a).

[28] Id. at §2000e-1(a).

[29] Id. at §2000e-2(e)(2).

[30] See EEOC v. Pacific Press Publ'g Ass'n, 676 F.2d 1272, 1276 (9th Cir. 1982); EEOC Notice N-915, September 23, 1987.

[31] H.R. 1755/S. 815, §6, 113th Cong. (citations omitted).

[32] See LeBoon v. Lancaster Jewish Cmty. Ctr. Ass'n, 503 F.3d 217, 226-27 (3rd Cir. 2007) (providing a summary discussion of circuit courts' interpretations of organizations that qualify under Title VII's exemption).

[33] Id.

[34] Id.

[35] Id. at 229-230.

[36] 859 F.2d 610 (9th Cir. 1988).

[37] Id. at 611-12 (internal quotations omitted).

[38] Id. at 618.

[39] Id. at 619.

[40] 585 F. Supp. 435 (N.D. Ill. 1984), aff'd, 803 F.2d 351 (7th Cir. 1986).

[41] Id. at 440-41.

[42] Id.

[43] 990 F.2d 458 (9th Cir. 1993).

[44] Id. at 462-63 (internal quotations omitted).

[45] Id. at 461, n. 7.

[46] 113 F.3d 196 (11th Cir. 1997).

[47] 42 U.S.C. §2000e-5(g).

[48] For more information, see CRS Report RL30470, Affirmative Action in Employment: A Legal Overview, by Jody Feder.

[49] 42 U.S.C. §1981a(b).

[50] Pollard v. E.I. du Pont de Nemours & Co., 532 U.S. 843 (2001).

[51] U.S. Const. amend. XI.

[52] U.S. Const. amend. XIV.

[53] 517 U.S. 44 (1996).

[54] 527 U.S. 706 (1999).

[55] 521 U.S. 507 (1997).

[56] Kimel v. Bd. of Regents, 528 U.S. 62 (2000).

[57] United States v. Morrison, 529 U.S. 598 (2000).

[58] Bd. of Trs. of the Univ. of Ala. v. Garrett, 531 U.S. 356 (2001).

[59] College Savings Bank v. Florida Prepaid Postsecondary Educ. Expense Bd., 527 U.S. 666, 686 (1999).

[60] U.S. Const. art. I, §8, cl. 1.

[61] Litman v. George Mason Univ., 186 F.3d 544, 555 (4th Cir. 1999). For more information on waiving state sovereign immunity, see CRS Report RL30315, Federalism, State Sovereignty, and the Constitution: Basis and Limits of Congressional Power, by Kenneth R. Thomas.

[62] 42 U.S.C. §2000e-5(k). See also, Albermarle Paper Co. v. Moody, 442 U.S. 405 (1975); New York Gaslight Club, Inc. v. Carey, 447 U.S. 54 (1980).

[63] Hensley v. Eckherhart, 461 U.S. 424 (1983).

[64] Christiansburg Garment Co. v. EEOC, 434 U.S. 412 (1978).

[65] 29 C.F.R. §1614.501.

INDEX

A

abuse, 49
access, 2, 5, 7, 26, 48
accountability, 49
accounting, 96
administrators, 101
adults, 11, 12, 15, 20, 35, 58, 60
affirmative action, 102
affirming, 20, 46
age, vii, 18, 25, 32, 35, 36, 61, 63
Age Discrimination in Employment Act, 103, 105
agencies, 2, 4, 5, 7, 10, 11, 12, 13, 16, 20, 23, 25, 26, 27, 31, 32, 33, 34, 37, 38, 39, 40, 41, 42, 43, 45, 46, 47, 48, 49, 51, 53, 58, 60, 61, 93, 102, 104
Air Force, 98
alcoholics, 11
ambassadors, 26
American History, 53
American Psychiatric Association, 6, 53
American Psychological Association, 53
Americans with Disabilities Act, 103
appropriations, 7, 10, 13, 54
arrest, 15
assessment, 17
atmosphere, 5
attitudes, 20, 21, 28, 29, 35, 36, 38, 39, 41, 43, 44, 49, 50, 58, 60
Attorney General, 23
authorities, 49
authority, 15, 22, 23, 26, 50, 95, 102, 104
awareness, 41

B

base, 87
behaviors, 14, 49
benefits, 20, 25, 26, 27, 28, 44, 50, 57, 58, 103
bias, 93
Bible, 101
bureaucracy, 19
Bush, President, 46
businesses, 28, 58

C

case law, 86, 87
causation, 105
challenges, 50
Chicago, 53, 100
children, 26, 27
CIA, 7, 16, 21
cities, 58
civil rights, 103
civil servants, 12, 14
civil service, 6, 7, 11, 12, 13, 16, 17, 19, 51
Civil Service Reform Act, 21

classes, 88
classification, 93
climate, 36, 44
Clinton, President William Jefferson (, 25, 56
clusters, 38, 43, 51
Coast Guard, 98
Code of Federal Regulations, 23
codes of conduct, 19
Cold War, 7, 53
collaboration, 39
collective bargaining, 61
color, vii, 25, 32, 61, 63, 93, 99
communication, 5, 39, 48, 49
communism, 6
Communist Party, 14
communities, 7
community, 22, 52, 100
compensation, 91, 92, 93
competition, 29
compliance, 98
composition, 100
conference, 22
confidentiality, 34
conflict, 18, 99
conformity, 96, 97, 99
Congress, 1, 6, 10, 12, 13, 32, 47, 61, 91, 92, 103
Congressional Accountability Act, 93
Constitution, 17, 56, 106
constitutional limitations, 103
construction, 94
convention, 101
conversations, 44
conviction, 15, 22
cost, 26
counseling, 26
Court of Appeals, 16, 61, 97, 100, 101
culture, 28, 31
curriculum, 98
customers, 28

D

damages, 102, 103
danger, 16
data set, 3, 35
defendants, 102
demographic data, 35
Department of Agriculture, 24, 61
Department of Health and Human Services, 43
Department of Justice, 23, 56, 102
Diagnostic and Statistical Manual of Mental Disorders, 6, 53
directives, 61
disability, vii, 25, 32, 34, 61, 63, 87, 89, 90
discomfort, 50
discrimination, vii, 2, 3, 4, 5, 6, 22, 23, 24, 25, 28, 29, 30, 31, 32, 33, 34, 36, 44, 45, 46, 47, 48, 49, 58, 59, 61, 63, 64, 65, 66, 67, 68, 69, 70, 71, 72, 73, 74, 75, 76, 77, 78, 79, 80, 81, 82, 83, 84, 85, 86, 87, 88, 89, 90, 91, 92, 93, 95, 96, 97, 98, 99, 102, 103, 104, 105
District of Columbia, 12, 16, 17, 18, 22, 28, 61, 87
diversity, 19, 27, 28, 41, 49, 50, 51
DOJ, 102
double counting, 88
drug abuse, 26
drug addict, 14
drug addiction, 14
due process, 17

E

education, 49, 53, 59, 101
educational institutions, 92, 98
EEOC, 25, 45, 47, 61, 92, 94, 97, 100, 101, 102, 104, 105, 106
elaboration, 102
emergency, 27
emotional stability, 10
employees, 2, 3, 4, 5, 6, 7, 10, 11, 12, 13, 14, 15, 16, 19, 20, 21, 22, 23, 24, 25, 26, 27, 28, 29, 30, 31, 32, 33, 34, 35, 36, 37, 38, 39, 41, 43, 44, 45, 46, 47, 48, 49, 50, 51, 52, 53, 56, 58, 59, 60, 61, 92, 93, 94, 96, 98, 99, 102, 103, 105

employers, 21, 26, 28, 91, 92, 93, 94, 98, 99, 102, 104
employment, vii, 2, 3, 5, 6, 7, 9, 10, 11, 12, 15, 16, 17, 18, 19, 20, 21, 22, 23, 25, 26, 27, 28, 30, 31, 32, 33, 36, 44, 45, 48, 51, 52, 53, 54, 55, 61, 63, 64, 65, 66, 67, 68, 69, 70, 71, 72, 73, 74, 75, 76, 77, 78, 79, 80, 81, 82, 83, 84, 85, 86, 87, 88, 89, 90,91, 92, 93, 94, 95, 96, 97, 98, 99, 100, 101, 102, 104, 105
employment status, 93
empowerment, 39
enforcement, 48, 97, 102
entrapment, 7
environment, 41
Equal Employment Opportunity Commission, 25, 57, 59, 61, 92, 100
equal opportunity, 51
equality, 25, 26, 28
equipment, 100
equity, 25
espionage, 14
evacuation, 26
evidence, 15, 16, 17, 18, 21, 23, 46, 54
evolution, 3
exclusion, 16
executive branch, 7, 13, 19, 87
executive order(s), 2, 13, 14, 25, 33, 45, 54, 56, 57, 62, 87
exercise, 98, 103
exercises, 102
exposure, 7, 10

F

factor analysis, 51, 52
Fair Labor Standards Act, 103
fairness, 28
faith, 100, 101
family members, 26
FBI, 12, 13, 14, 21, 53
fear, 7, 20, 36, 41
Federal Bureau of Investigation (FBI), 6, 14
federal courts, 96, 97, 102
federal employment, 104
Federal Government, vii, 3, 6, 11, 14, 16, 20, 25, 26, 27, 45, 51, 53, 56, 57, 61, 62, 91, 92
federal law, 63, 103
femininity, 96
fiber, 10
financial, 99, 103, 104
financial support, 99
fires, 97
First Amendment, 24
fiscal year, 87, 88, 89, 90
fitness, 17, 21, 22
focus groups, 49
Ford, 105
foreign intelligence, 7
Fourteenth Amendment, 103
fringe benefits, 93, 102
funds, 15, 103

G

GAO, 58, 63, 86
gay men, 31, 58
gender identity, vii, 28, 36, 48, 49, 52, 59, 64, 65, 66, 67, 68, 69, 70, 71, 72, 73, 74, 75, 76, 77, 78, 79, 80, 81, 82, 83, 84, 85, 86, 87, 88, 89, 90, 91, 92, 93, 94, 96, 97, 99, 102, 103
gender stereotyping, 47, 95, 98
General Services Administration (GSA), 41
genetic information, 61
Georgia, 97
God, 100
grants, 27, 104
GSA, 42
guidance, 25, 27, 33, 46, 49, 86, 87
guidelines, 21

H

harassment, 95, 96
Hawaii, 64, 87, 88
health, 27
health insurance, 27

heterosexuality, 95, 105
heterosexuals, 11
HHS, 43, 44
hiring, 10, 20, 91, 92, 93, 99, 100, 102
history, 4, 5, 13, 30, 48, 91, 92, 100, 102
HIV, 28
HIV/AIDS, 28
homosexuality, 6, 8, 10, 12, 17, 19, 22, 23, 53, 95, 96, 99, 105
homosexuals, 6, 7, 10, 11, 12, 13, 14, 15, 16, 18, 19, 20
House, 1, 6, 22, 45, 46, 53
House of Representatives, 1, 22, 45, 46
human, 36, 37, 49, 60
human capital, 37
human resources, 36, 49
hysteria, 12

I

ideals, 50
identity, 44, 64, 65, 87, 88, 89, 90, 91, 92, 94, 96, 98, 99, 100
image, 90
immunity, 103, 106
incidence, 30, 49
income, 26
independence, 20
individual character, 45
individual characteristics, 45
individual differences, 50
individuals, vii, 3, 4, 8, 10, 14, 20, 28, 31, 36, 44, 47, 50, 52, 53, 58, 59, 60, 64, 87, 89, 94, 96, 98, 103
injury, 31, 103
integrity, 21, 49
intelligence, 7
intrinsic motivation, 31
Iowa, 72, 87, 89
Iron Curtain, 7
issues, 2, 5, 10, 28, 41, 48, 49, 50, 59, 87, 89

J

Jewish Community, 100
job performance, 2, 3, 17, 22, 23
jurisdiction, 61, 102

L

law enforcement, 14
laws, 4, 12, 15, 18, 22, 28, 30, 61, 64, 98
lawyers, 54
lead, 24, 47, 48, 51
leadership, 36, 39
learning, 14, 99
legal protection, 104
legislation, 2, 5, 12, 25, 33, 45, 48, 61, 91, 92, 93, 94, 98, 99, 102, 103, 105
liberty, 19, 56
light, 10, 87, 105
litigation, 23, 58, 104
local government, 87, 102
long-term care insurance, 27
loyalty, 13, 54

M

major issues, 12
majority, 17, 19, 28, 96
malfeasance, 93
management, 2, 5, 8, 21, 22, 23, 37, 39, 45, 48, 49, 51, 60, 100
manufacturing, 100
marital status, 2, 4, 29, 30, 32
marriage, 28
Maryland, 87, 89
matter, 21
medical, 15, 27, 28
membership, 14, 93
mental disorder, 6, 53
mental health, 53
mental illness, 14
mentoring, 41, 49
Mexico, 87
military, 98, 105

minorities, 28, 41
mission, 99, 100
Missouri, 53
morality, 12, 17

N

National Aeronautics and Space Administration, 39
national origin, vii, 2, 4, 25, 29, 30, 32, 61, 63, 93, 99
national security, 13, 14
National Security Agency, 14
National Security Council, 14
negative effects, 32
negativity, 51
neutral, 94
New Deal, 54
NSA, 14

O

Obama, President Barack, 26
obstacles, 27
officials, 6, 11, 12, 24, 64, 87
openness, 16
operations, 23, 100
opportunities, 93
organizational culture, 45
orientation discrimination, 2, 4, 5, 22, 25, 28, 29, 30, 31, 33, 45, 46, 47, 48, 95
OSC, 22, 23, 24, 46, 48, 56
overlap, 64
oversight, 60
ownership, 99, 101

P

Pacific, 105, 106
parallel, 25, 47, 94, 102
participants, 12, 18
Pentagon, 7
performance ratings, 23
permit, 96
personal life, 44
personality, 19
physical abuse, 95
pilot study, 34
police, 11, 14, 97
policy, vii, 2, 3, 5, 15, 18, 20, 21, 23, 25, 28, 33, 45, 48, 60, 86, 102, 105
political leaders, 6
political system, 13
population, 28, 35
positive attitudes, 37, 43, 44
PPP, 3, 4, 5, 21, 22, 23, 24, 30, 31, 32, 33, 46, 48
precedent, 100, 101
preferential treatment, 94, 102
president, 1, 6, 13, 14, 21, 25, 26, 46, 56, 57, 101
prevention, 28
prima facie, 97
principles, 24, 25
private schools, 101
private sector, 26, 27, 91, 92, 104
private sector employers, 91, 92
probability, 31
profit, 100
propagation, 98
proposed regulations, 23
protection, 16, 28, 45, 64, 65, 66, 67, 68, 69, 70, 71, 72, 73, 74, 75, 76, 77, 78, 79, 80, 81, 82, 83, 84, 85, 86, 95, 98, 99, 103
psychiatry, 53
public employment, 17
public interest, 16, 104
public service, 18, 27

Q

questionnaire, 52, 65, 87
quotas, 92, 94, 102

R

race, vii, 25, 32, 61, 63, 93, 99
reading, 102

reality, 39
reasoning, 16, 95
recall, 93
recognition, 24
recommendations, 51, 52, 54
recruiting, 41
regulations, 8, 9, 18, 23, 26, 32, 33, 47, 59, 86, 87
rehabilitation, 15
relatives, 27
reliability, 20
relief, 102
religion, vii, 25, 32, 34, 61, 63, 93, 98, 99, 100
religious beliefs, 99, 100
reputation, 21
requirement(s), 1, 11, 14, 21, 30, 33, 94, 99
researchers, 45
resolution, 47, 53, 102
resources, 39
response, 4, 7, 12, 13, 17, 20, 26, 30, 34, 52, 58, 64
retaliation, 32, 47, 94, 105
retirement, 27
revenue, 101
rhetoric, 10
rights, 2, 3, 6, 24, 25, 28, 32, 45, 47, 51, 59, 96, 98
risk(s), 10, 11, 12, 18
rules, 11, 18
Russia, 53

S

sabotage, 14
school, 99, 101
Schwarzenegger, California Governor, 55
scope, 45, 59, 87, 92, 95, 98, 103, 104
security, 10, 11, 12, 16, 41, 56
security threats, 41
self-image, 89, 90
Senate, 1, 6, 7, 11, 15, 22, 24, 25, 46, 54, 61, 63, 92, 94
services, 7, 28, 92, 99, 100, 101
settlements, 102
sex, vii, 7, 8, 10, 11, 12, 14, 20, 24, 25, 26, 27, 28, 32, 34, 47, 52, 54, 61, 63, 87, 88, 89, 90, 93, 95, 96, 97, 99, 105
sexual behavior, 15, 20
sexual harassment, 47, 95
sexual orientation, vii, 1, 2, 3, 4, 5, 6, 20, 22, 23, 24, 25, 27, 28, 29, 30, 31, 32, 33, 34, 36, 44, 45, 46, 47, 48, 49, 51, 52, 56, 59, 60, 64, 65, 66, 67, 68, 69, 70, 71, 72, 73, 74, 75, 76, 77, 78, 79, 80, 81, 82, 83, 84, 85, 86, 87, 88, 89, 90, 91, 92, 93, 94, 95, 96,99, 102, 103, 105
sexuality, 56
showing, 15, 23
signs, 4
society, 12, 15, 51, 98, 99, 101
Soviet Union, 7, 14
spending, 103
Spring, 56
state(s), 17, 21, 25, 45, 51, 64, 65, 87, 88, 89, 90, 94, 96, 97, 98, 102, 103, 104, 105, 106
statistics, 59, 88, 94
statutes, 64, 87, 90, 94
statutory provisions, 64, 65, 87
stereotypes, 48, 96
stereotyping, 98
stigmatized, 17
structure, 22
styles, 54
subsistence, 27
supervisor(s), 4, 24, 29, 32, 33, 34, 35, 39, 49, 50, 59, 97
Supreme Court, 27, 47, 95, 96, 97, 102, 103, 105

T

talent, 28
target, 4
teachers, 7, 101
telephone, 58
temperature, 41
time frame, 87
Title I, 59